CARIBBEAN
COOKING

THE BOOK OF
CARIBBEAN
COOKING

LESLEY MACKLEY

PHOTOGRAPHED BY
PATRICK McLEAVEY

HPBooks

ANOTHER BESTSELLING VOLUME FROM HPBOOKS

HPBooks
Published by The Berkley Publishing Group
A division of Penguin Putnam Inc.
375 Hudson Street
New York, New York 10014

Home Economist: Alison Austin

Notice: The information contained in this book is true and
complete to the best of our knowledge. All
recommendations are made without any guarantee on the
part of the author or the publisher. The author and the
publisher disclaim all liability in connection with the use of
this information.

First edition: March 2000

The Penguin Putnam Inc. World Wide Web site address is
http://www.penguinputnam.com

This book has been cataloged with the Library of Congress.

ISBN 1-55788-328-9(tp)

Printed and bound in Spain

10 9 8 7 6 5 4 3 2 1

CONTENTS

FOREWORD

The cooking of the Caribbean is a happy blend of different styles that have developed from the varied culinary traditions of the many nationalities who have settled in the islands over the centuries. This ethnic diversity, combined with the region's climate and agriculture, has created a cuisine of vibrant flavors that match the intensity of the tropical sun.

The Caribbean diet is varied and healthy, being based on an abundance of fresh fruit and vegetables and plentiful supplies of fish and shellfish. Caribbean cooking is simple, colorful and full of the flavors of aromatic spices, hot pepper sauces, fragrant marinades and fiery spice rubs.

The Caribbean is now a popular holiday destination and more people are discovering the delights of West Indian cuisine. Further inspiration comes from television programmes that encourage cooks to try dishes at home and, luckily, this has never been easier. Tropical fruits and vegetables, and exotic fish, are becoming readily available in shops and supermarkets.

The Book of Caribbean Cooking contains over 80 recipes, from snacks and appetizers to exotic cocktails. Some dishes are traditional while some are modern variations on traditional themes, reflecting current trends but using Caribbean ingredients and influences. Many of the recipes are suitable for vegetarians. Whether cooking for the family or entertaining friends, the recipes in this book will transport you to a tropical paradise and your cooking will never be the same again.

INTRODUCTION

In 1492, when Christopher Columbus discovered the islands of the Caribbean, which stretch from Florida to Venezuela, he thought that he had found Paradise. He brought back to Europe news of a bright and colorful land alive with abundant flowers, juicy tropical fruits, the sound of birdsong, and the scent of spices.

The cuisine of the 200 islands of the Caribbean is a mixture of so many styles that it is almost impossible to define it.

The original inhabitants of the islands were Amerindians - Arawaks and Caribs. The Arawaks, who were the first arrivals, were skilled farmers. They brought with them maize, chili peppers, yams, sweet potatoes, and cassava, and gathered wild fruit such as guavas and pineapples. The Caribs were natural hunters who lived mainly by fishing and hunting, and eventually eliminated the Arawaks. The early Spanish settlers introduced many fruits and vegetables, such as limes, mangoes, coconut, sugar cane, coffee, ginger, tamarind, and rice, and their influence is still seen in much Caribbean cooking today.

In the sixteenth century, African slaves, who were brought in to work in the sugar plantations, introduced okra and black-eyed beans, or peas as they are often called, and Indian workers brought curries and chutneys. Together with Chinese settlers and Jewish people from Portugal, these immigrants have all left their mark.

During the seventeenth and eighteenth centuries European nations were establishing New World empires. Constant warfare meant that some islands frequently changed hands and each time the culinary traditions of the previous occupiers were left behind.

Certain basic styles bring together both the diverse ingredients and the cooking methods from Europe, Asia, and Africa, but each national group of islands has its own characteristics and individual flavors.

The cooking of the Caribbean is based on abundant tropical fruit and vegetables, and large catches of fish and shellfish. Meals tend to be made with recipes that have been handed down through the generations. Most cooks have their own secret ingredients which make their recipes unique. Soups and stews containing plenty of vegetables, cooked and served in one pot, are favorite dishes, and are often served with dumplings. Cooking over an open fire is common, with meat and fish being marinated in hot spice mixtures. Rice is an important food and is served at almost every meal with meat, fish, or vegetables.

Goat, pork, and chicken are the most frequently eaten meats, although nowadays a certain amount of beef is imported. Pork is widely used and no part of the animal goes to waste. Pigs' heads, tails, and trotters, often pickled and dyed bright crimson, are frequently seen in the markets: pickling originated in the days before refrigeration when it was used as a way of preserving meat in the hot climate. Stuffed roast suckling pig is served on special occasions, traditionally accompanied by boiled or roast yams and sweet potatoes.

There is a plentiful supply of fish in the seas around the islands and fish is eaten everywhere. Fishermen bring in crayfish, shrimp, crabs, flying fish, grouper, red snapper, tuna, and kingfish. Mackerel is cheap and very widely used. As with meat, salting was a method of preserving fish before refrigeration, and salt cod is still a national dish.

The range of vegetables is enormous with root vegetables such as yams, cassava, and sweet potatoes being great favorites. Vegetables are often stuffed or made into stews or curries. Pumpkin is very popular and is eaten both as a vegetable or incorporated into sweet dishes. Pulses are served as accompaniments, made into soups, added to stews, and combined with rice in the traditional dish: rice and peas. West Indian fruits have become more familiar in the West in recent years. Mangoes, fresh coconuts, and plantains are all familiar sights in Western shops.

Herbs and spices season most dishes. Meat, chicken, and fish are often marinated in a spicy mixture before cooking. As well as adding flavor, marinating also helps to tenderize meat. Chilies are widely used. Whole

chilies are sometimes cooked in a dish then removed before serving. Allspice, cloves, and cinnamon are popular spices, and thyme and cilantro are the most widely used herbs.

Sugar cane is grown in many islands and sugar is cheap throughout the Caribbean; most of the islanders like very sweet desserts and drinks. Rum is produced from sugar cane and is either drunk as it is - dark, white, or golden - or forms the basis of punches and cocktails. Other favorite drinks are ginger beer, fresh fruit juices, sweet fruit syrups, sweet coffee, and weak tea.

The natural abundance of fresh fruit and vegetables and the plentiful supplies of fish, combined with the varied culinary traditions of the many nationalities who have settled in the islands over the centuries, make Caribbean cooking a fascinating melting pot of flavors from both East and West.

CARIBBEAN INGREDIENTS

ACKEES
The edible part of the ackee fruit resembles scrambled egg in appearance, and has a delicate flavor; it is available canned. Ackees are an essential ingredient of the popular Jamaican dish, saltfish and ackees.

ALLSPICE
Also known as pimento or Jamaican pepper, allspice is the dried fruit of the pimento tree. The dried berries look like peppercorns and have a flavor of cloves, cinnamon, and nutmeg. Allspice is used whole or ground in many dishes.

ARROWROOT
A white starchy powder used for thickening sauces, and also used in place of flour in baking.

BREADFRUIT
Breadfruit are large green fruits about 12in (30cm) in diameter. They have a pale yellow flesh similar to a potato. Breadfruit is only edible when cooked and can be used instead of potato, rice, or pasta as an accompaniment to any dish. Fresh breadfruit are not widely available, but canned breadfruit are an excellent substitute.

CALLALOO
The leaves of two distinct plants, the taro plant and Chinese spinach, which are used interchangeably, though the taro plant is most widely used. Its tubers are also popular in Island cooking and may be known as coco or dasheen. Callaloo looks like spinach and is used in similar ways. It has given its name to the most famous of Caribbean soups.

CHAYOTE
Also known as cho-cho or chrostophene, chayote is a type of pear-shaped squash that is often covered in prickly hairs, and best when dark green. The firm, delicately flavored flesh is often sliced and fried in batter. Young chayote shoots are eaten like asparagus. The leaves are eaten as greens and the large tuberous roots are treated like yams.

CHILI PEPPERS
The use of chilies is widespread in Caribbean cooking. The hot Scotch bonnet is the most popular variety; it is a small, lantern-shaped chili varying in color from pale yellow to bright red. Chilies are also available in the form of relishes, crushed and bottled in vinegar, or in the form of hot pepper sauces and chili powder.

COCONUT
The liquid inside a fresh coconut is known as coconut water or juice, and can be drunk by itself or as a mixer with gin, vodka, or rum; it is never used in cooking. Coconut milk is the liquid produced by pressing the flesh of fresh coconuts after the shell, husk, and juice have been removed. Available in cans, coconut milk is widely used in Caribbean recipes. Creamed coconut is pure fresh coconut formed into a block, and provides a convenient alternative to either fresh or unsweetened flaked coconut. Creamed coconut is either added directly to dishes, or dissolved in water to give a substitute for coconut milk. Cartons of coconut cream, which is smoother and richer than milk or creamed coconut, have recently become available.

CORNMEAL
Also known as polenta or maize meal, cornmeal is yellow maize that has been either coarsely or finely ground. Coarse and fine cornmeal can be used interchangeable, depending upon the texture required. Cornmeal is used in cornbreads, cakes, muffins, dumplings, and puddings; it also gives a crisp coating to fried foods.

GUAVAS
The fruit of an evergreen tree, guavas are about 5in (12.5cm) in diameter with pale yellow skins and pink or white flesh that has a gritty texture and is pitted with hundreds of tiny, hard seeds. Guavas may be eaten raw but their flavor improves with cooking. They make excellent jams, jellies, and pastes. Guavas are available canned.

GUNGO PEAS
Gungo peas, which are also known as pigeon peas, are popular in West Indian cooking and are used fresh, dried, and canned.

OKRA

Alternative names for okra include bamies, gumbo, and ladies' fingers. Green okra pods are prized for the slippery texture that they give to soups and stews.

PAPAYA

Papaya, which can also be called papaw, is the fruit of a woody herbaceous plant. Unripe papaya is hard and green and is used as a vegetable, or for relishes and chutneys. Papaya ripens to yellow tinged with orange, with vivid salmon pink flesh surrounding a cluster of gray-black, edible seeds. Ripe papaya is used in both sweet and savory dishes.

PLANTAIN

A large member of the banana family, plantains must be cooked before being eaten. Plantains are used green and unripe, or when ripened until the skin turns black. They have a mild, squash-like flavor and are widely used in West Indian cooking for both sweet and savory dishes.

SALT CODFISH

Although fresh fish is readily available, salt codfish is still popular on all the islands. Salt codfish must be thoroughly soaked before cooking. Sometimes other fish are salted.

SWEET POTATOES

The sweet potato is an elongated, edible tuber but is not related to the ordinary potato. Orange-fleshed sweet potatoes have a pinkish-purple skin and a dense texture with a sweet, chestnut flavor. The white-fleshed variety has a milder taste. Sweet potatoes can be baked, fried, steamed, or boiled, although boiling can make them rather watery.

YAMS

Yams are edible tubers and come in a wide variety of shapes and sizes; they have white or yellow flesh and a nutty flavor. Yams are cooked in the same ways as potatoes. Yams should not be confused with the yellow-fleshed sweet potato which is sometimes known as the Louisiana yam.

CALLALOO

1lb (450g) callaloo leaves or spinach
2 tablespoons (1oz/25g) butter
1 onion, finely chopped
2 cloves garlic, crushed
4oz (115g) okra, sliced
1 sprig thyme
3¾ cups (30fl oz/850ml) chicken or vegetable stock
14fl oz (400ml) can coconut milk
salt and freshly ground black pepper
8oz (225g) fresh, canned, or frozen crabmeat
hot pepper sauce, to taste
finely diced red capsicum, to garnish

Finely shred the callaloo or spinach leaves.

In a large pan, heat butter, add onion and garlic and cook for 10 minutes until soft and golden. Add okra and thyme and cook, stirring, for 5 minutes. Stir in callaloo or spinach then add stock, coconut milk, and seasoning. Bring to the boil, cover, and simmer gently for 15 minutes.

Add crabmeat and cook gently for 5 more minutes. Add hot pepper sauce to taste. Ladle into heated soup bowls and garnish with diced red capsicum.

Serves 6

SUNSHINE SOUP

2 tablespoons (1oz/25g) butter
1 large onion, roughly chopped
1 celery stick, finely chopped
2lb (1kg) pumpkin, peeled, deseeded, and cubed
1 small red chili, deseeded and finely chopped
3¾ cups (30fl oz/850ml) chicken or vegetable stock
14fl oz (400ml) can coconut milk
1 tablespoon lime juice
salt and freshly ground black pepper
¼ teaspoon grated nutmeg
toasted coconut flakes and lime rind, to garnish

In a large saucepan, heat butter, add onion and celery, and cook gently for 10 minutes until soft.

Add pumpkin, chili, stock, coconut milk, lime juice, and seasoning, and bring to the boil. Cover and simmer gently for 20-30 minutes until pumpkin is soft. Purée soup in a blender or food processor then return to pan.

Reheat soup, if necessary, and stir in nutmeg. Serve in warmed soup bowls, garnished with coconut flakes and lime rind.

Serves 6

Note: Any type of squash, such as butternut, may be used instead of pumpkin.

SWEET POTATO & TOMATO SOUP

1 tablespoon oil
1 tablespoon (½ oz/15g) butter
2 onions, finely chopped
2 sticks celery, thinly sliced
8oz (225g) sweet potatoes, diced
14oz (400g) can chopped tomatoes
grated rind and juice of 1 orange
3¼ cups (30fl oz/850ml) chicken or vegetable stock
½ teaspoon chopped fresh thyme
1 teaspoon chopped fresh oregano
salt and freshly ground black pepper
sour cream, orange rind, and cayenne pepper, to
  garnish

In a saucepan, heat oil and butter. Add onions and celery and cook for 10 minutes.

Add sweet potatoes, tomatoes, orange rind and juice, stock, thyme, oregano, and seasoning. Bring to the boil, cover, and simmer for 20 minutes until sweet potatoes are soft.

Purée soup, in batches if necessary, in a blender or food processor. Return to pan and heat through. Serve in warmed bowls, garnished with a swirl of sour cream, and sprinkled with orange rind and cayenne pepper.

Serves 6

FISH SOUP

2 tablespoons oil
1 onion, finely chopped
1 green capsicum, finely chopped
2 cloves garlic, crushed
2lb (1kg) tomatoes, peeled and chopped
2 teaspoons tomato paste
2½ cups (20fl oz/550ml) fish stock
1¼ cups (10fl oz/300ml) dry white wine
salt and freshly ground black pepper
2 teaspoons arrowroot
1lb (450g) firm white fish, cubed
4 tablespoons chopped fresh parsley
4oz (115g) cooked, peeled shrimp

Heat oil in a large pan. Cook onion, green capsicum, and garlic for 10 minutes.

Add tomatoes, tomato paste, stock, wine, and seasoning. Bring to the boil, cover and simmer for 10 minutes. Blend arrowroot with a little water and stir into soup. Add fish and 3 tablespoons of the parsley, and cook gently for 5 minutes until fish is just cooked but not breaking up.

Add shrimp and cook for 2 minutes longer until heated through. Serve in warmed soup bowls, garnished with the reserved parsley.

Serves 4-6

PLANTAIN CRISPS & AVOCADO DIP

3 ripe plantains, peeled
oil, for deep frying
sea salt
pinch of chili powder
AVOCADO DIP:
flesh from 2 ripe avocados
2 scallions, finely chopped
1 clove garlic, crushed
1 tablespoon lime juice
4 tablespoons mayonnaise
hot pepper sauce, to taste
salt and freshly ground black pepper
paprika, to garnish

Cut off both ends of plantains, and slice as thinly as possible.

Half fill a saucepan or deep-fat fryer with oil and heat to 375F (190C) until a cube of bread browns in 40 seconds. Deep-fry the plantain slices in batches for 2 minutes until crisp and golden. Drain on paper towels. Sprinkle with salt and chili powder and leave to cool.

To make avocado dip, place avocado flesh in a blender or food processor with scallions, garlic, lime juice, mayonnaise, pepper sauce, and seasoning, and process until well blended. Transfer to a bowl and sprinkle with paprika. Serve with plantain crisps.

Serves 6

— STAMP & GO (FISH FRITTERS) —

1 cup (4oz/115g) self-rising flour
salt
1 egg, beaten
¾ cup (6fl oz/175ml) milk
1 tablespoon (½ oz/15g) butter, melted
8oz (225g) salt cod, soaked overnight
1 tablespoon oil
1 onion, finely chopped
1 fresh red chili, deseeded and finely chopped
oil, for frying
lemon wedges, to garnish

Sift flour and salt into a bowl. Mix together egg, milk, and melted butter, and stir into flour. Mix well to a smooth batter; add a little more milk if necessary. Allow to stand.

Meanwhile, drain and rinse salt cod. Place in a large saucepan, cover with cold water, and bring to the boil. Reduce heat, cover, and simmer for 20 minutes until tender. Drain and cool. Discard skin and any bones, and flake flesh. Heat oil in a skillet, add onion, and cook for 10 minutes until soft. Allow to cool slightly.

Stir the fish, onion, and chili into the batter. Heat about ½in (1cm) oil in a skillet. Drop spoonfuls of batter mixture into oil, a few at a time. Fry for about 2 minutes on each side until crisp and golden. Serve with lemon wedges.

Serves 6

VARIATION: Although these little fritters are traditionally made with salt cod, cooked fresh cod may be used instead.

— PRAWN & POTATO BALLS —

1lb (450g) potatoes, diced
3 tablespoons (1½ oz/40g) butter
2 egg yolks, beaten
2oz (50g) Cheddar cheese, grated
1 tablespoon chopped fresh cilantro
6 scallions, finely chopped
1lb (450g) peeled shrimp, roughly chopped
½ teaspoon hot pepper sauce
salt and freshly ground black pepper
all-purpose flour, for coating
1 egg, beaten
½ cup (2oz/50g) dry bread crumbs
oil, for deep frying
LIME MAYONNAISE:
¾ cup (6fl oz/175ml) mayonnaise
1 tablespoon lime juice

Place potatoes in a saucepan, cover with cold salted water, and bring to the boil. Simmer, covered, for 15 minutes until tender. Drain and mash with butter, egg yolks, and cheese. Leave to cool. Stir in cilantro, scallions, shrimp, hot pepper sauce, and seasoning. Form into 30 small balls and arrange on a non-stick baking sheet. Chill for 30 minutes. To make lime mayonnaise, mix together mayonnaise and lime juice, and set aside.

Roll shrimp balls in flour, then in beaten egg, then in bread crumbs. Half-fill a deep-fat fryer with oil and heat to 375F (190C) until a cube of bread browns in 40 seconds. Deep-fry balls in hot oil in batches for 5 minutes until golden brown. Drain on paper towels and keep warm while cooking remaining balls, then serve immediately with lime mayonnaise.

Makes 30

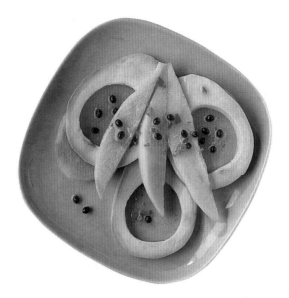

— AVOCADO & PAPAYA SALAD —

2 small papayas
2 avocados, peeled and sliced lengthwise
DRESSING:
2 tablespoons lime juice
1 teaspoon sugar
⅓ cup (2½fl oz/70ml) olive oil
1 fresh red chili, deseeded and finely chopped
1 teaspoon Dijon mustard
salt and freshly ground black pepper

Peel papayas and cut in half lengthwise. Remove seeds and reserve. Thinly slice papayas and arrange with avocado slices on 4 individual plates.

To make dressing, put lime juice, sugar, olive oil, chili, mustard, and seasoning in a bowl and whisk together.

Pour dressing over salads and scatter a few of the reserved papaya seeds over, to garnish. Serve immediately.

Serves 4

PLANTAIN, CORN, & CHILI CAKES

8oz (225g) peeled ripe plantain, grated
½ cup (3oz/85g) cornmeal, sifted
1 egg, beaten
¼ cup (2fl oz/50ml) Caribbean beer
1 teaspoon lime juice
4 scallions, chopped
2 tablespoons chopped fresh cilantro
1 fresh green chili, deseeded and finely chopped
salt
oil, for frying
sliced scallions, to garnish
crème fraîche, to serve

Put plantain, cornmeal, egg, beer, lime juice, scallions, cilantro, chili, and salt into a bowl and mix thoroughly. Leave for 15 minutes.

Heat ¼in (5mm) oil in a skillet. Add spoonfuls of mixture and fry, in batches, for 1½ minutes on each side until golden brown. Drain on paper towels and keep warm while frying remaining cakes.

Garnish cakes with scallions and serve immediately with crème fraîche.

Makes 20 small cakes

NOTE: These cakes tend to burn easily, so watch them carefully, and lower heat, if necessary.

ACKEE & SALTFISH

8oz (225g) salt cod, soaked overnight and drained
4 slices bacon
2 tablespoons oil
1 onion, chopped
1 green capsicum, quartered and sliced
4 scallions, sliced
2 green chilies, deseeded and finely chopped
3 tomatoes, peeled and chopped
freshly ground black pepper
2 tablespoons chopped fresh parsley
19oz (538g) can ackees, drained
1 tablespoon (½oz/15g) butter
1 ripe plantain, peeled and sliced lengthwise

Preheat broiler. Put fish in a saucepan, cover with cold water, and bring to boil. Cover and simmer for 20 minutes.

Drain fish, and remove skin and bone. Flake flesh and set aside. Broil bacon until crisp. Drain on paper towels and chop. In a skillet, heat oil. Add onion and cook for 5 minutes. Add green capsicum, scallions, and chilies, and cook for 5 minutes until soft. Add tomatoes, pepper, and parsley and cook for a few minutes until well blended. Add fish, ackees, and bacon, and stir very gently until heated through.

Heat butter in a skillet, add plantain slices, and cook for 2-3 minutes on each side. Drain on paper towels. Serve fish and ackees garnished with the fried plantain as a main course with Rice and Peas (see page 61).

Serves 4

——— ESCOVITCH MACKEREL ———

8 fresh mackerel fillets
juice of 1 lime
salt and freshly ground black pepper
2 green capsicums, sliced
2 onions, thinly sliced
2 carrots, thinly sliced
6 black peppercorns
small piece mace blade
1 bay leaf
1 dried red chili
salt
5 tablespoons olive oil
6 tablespoons white wine vinegar
seasoned flour, for dusting
pimento-stuffed olives, sliced, and lime wedges, to
 garnish

Place fish in shallow, non-metallic dish. Pour lime juice over and add seasoning. Leave for 20 minutes. In a saucepan, put capsicums, onions, carrots, peppercorns, mace, bay leaf, chili, salt, and 2¼ cups (18fl oz/500ml) water. Bring to the boil, cover, and simmer for 30 minutes. Add 2 tablespoons of the olive oil, and the vinegar, and simmer for a further 2 minutes.

Pat fish dry with paper towels then dust with seasoned flour. Heat remaining oil in a skillet and fry fish fillets gently, in batches if necessary, for 4-5 minutes on each side. Transfer to a serving dish. Pour sauce over fish and leave to cool completely before serving, garnished with sliced olives and lime wedges.

Serves 2 as main course, 4 as an appetizer

VARIATION: Firm white fish can replace the mackerel.

— MUSSELS IN COCONUT SAUCE —

2lb (900g) mussels
1 tablespoon oil
2 shallots, finely chopped
1 clove garlic, crushed
4oz (115g) creamed coconut
½ cup (4fl oz/115ml) dry white wine
⅓ cup (3fl oz/85ml) heavy cream
1 teaspoon sugar
salt and freshly ground black pepper
1 teaspoon fresh thyme leaves
thyme sprigs, to garnish

Scrub mussels and remove their 'beards'.
Discard any that are damaged, unusually
heavy or remain open when tapped sharply.

In a large saucepan, heat oil. Add shallots
and garlic, and cook gently for 5 minutes
until soft. Crumble in creamed coconut and
add wine, cream, sugar, seasoning, and
thyme. Bring to boil, then reduce heat and
simmer gently for 5 minutes.

Add mussels and cook for 5 minutes until
they open; discard any that remain closed.
Serve in warmed, large soup plates and
garnish with thyme sprigs.

Serves 4

CRAB BACKS

¼ cup (2oz/50g) butter
1 onion, finely chopped
4 small, dressed crabs, each weighing about
   12oz (350g)
1 fresh red chili, deseeded and finely chopped
1½ cups (3oz/85g) fresh white bread crumbs
2 tablespoons chopped fresh chives
2 tablespoons chopped fresh parsley
2 cloves garlic, crushed
1 tablespoon lemon juice
3 tablespoons dark rum
¼ teaspoon grated nutmeg
salt and freshly ground black pepper
lemon wedges, to garnish

Preheat oven to 350F (180C). In a skillet, heat half the butter, add onion and cook for 10 minutes until soft. In a bowl, mix together crabmeat, chili, 1 cup (2oz/50g) of the bread crumbs, the chives, parsley, garlic, lemon juice, rum, nutmeg, and seasoning.

Spoon mixture into crab shells. Sprinkle remaining bread crumbs over crab filling and dot with remaining butter. Bake for 25-30 minutes until golden brown. Garnish with lemon wedges and serve with green salad.

Serves 4

NOTE: If fresh dressed crabs are not available, use fresh, frozen or canned crabmeat and bake in scallop shells or ramekins.

SEAFOOD & RICE

2 tablespoons olive oil
1 onion, finely chopped
1 clove garlic, crushed
2 tomatoes, peeled and chopped
generous pinch saffron threads
2 cups (12oz/350g) long grain rice
2½ cups (20fl oz/550ml) chicken stock
1 teaspoon hot pepper sauce
salt and freshly ground black pepper
1 tablespoon chopped fresh parsley
1 tablespoon chopped fresh cilantro
8oz (225g) frozen peas
14oz (400g) package frozen seafood mixture, thawed
GARNISH:
shrimp in shells
cilantro sprigs

In a large pan, heat oil. Add onion and garlic, and cook for 10 minutes until soft. Add tomatoes, saffron, and rice and cook for 5 minutes, stirring. Stir in stock, hot pepper sauce, and seasoning and bring to the boil. Lower the heat, cover and simmer for 15 minutes.

Carefully stir in parsley, cilantro, peas, and seafood. Cook, covered, for 10 minutes until peas and seafood have heated through, the rice is tender, and liquid has been absorbed. Add a little water if rice is too dry, or cook a little longer if all the stock has not been absorbed. Garnish with shrimp and cilantro sprigs.

Serves 4

TUNA BULJOLS

4 scallions, coarsely chopped
1 small onion, finely chopped
1 green capsicum, finely chopped
3 tomatoes, chopped
2 hard-cooked eggs, peeled and chopped
1 fresh red chili, deseeded and finely chopped
6 pitted green olives, coarsely chopped
1 tablespoon capers
2 tablespoons chopped fresh parsley
3 tablespoons olive oil
juice of 1 lime
salt and freshly ground black pepper
14oz (400g) can tuna, drained and coarsely flaked
lettuce leaves OR crackers, to serve

Put scallions, onion, green capsicum, tomatoes, eggs, chili, and olives in a large bowl.

Add capers, parsley, olive oil, lime juice, seasoning, and tuna. Carefully stir together. Cover and refrigerate overnight. Serve piled either on lettuce leaves or crackers.

Serves 4

NOTE: Buljols is traditionally made with soaked and cooked salt cod.

CRABCAKES WITH CHILI SALSA

1lb (450g) fresh, dressed brown and white crabmeat
4 scallions, finely chopped
1in (2.5cm) piece fresh root ginger, grated
2 tablespoons chopped fresh cilantro
2 tablespoons mayonnaise
1 teaspoon hot pepper sauce
salt and freshly ground black pepper
1-2 cups (2-4oz/50-115g) fresh bread crumbs
oil, for frying
CHILI SALSA:
4 tomatoes, peeled and finely diced
2 fresh red chilies, deseeded and finely chopped
1 small red onion, finely chopped
juice of 1 lime
3 tablespoons chopped fresh cilantro
salt and sugar

To make chili salsa, in a bowl, combine tomatoes, chilies, onion, lime juice, cilantro, and salt and sugar, to taste. Set aside. In a bowl, mix together crabmeat, scallions, ginger, cilantro, mayonnaise, hot pepper sauce, and seasoning. Stir in enough bread crumbs to make a mixture that is firm enough to form patties, but is not too stiff. Chill for 30 minutes.

Form crab mixture into 12 cakes. In a skillet, heat a shallow layer of oil and fry crab cakes, in batches if necessary, for 3-4 minutes on each side until browned. Drain on paper towels. Serve with chilled chili salsa.

Serves 4

NOTE: Fresh crabmeat will have the best flavor, but if it is not available, use frozen or canned crabmeat.

— MARINATED TUNA STEAKS —

4 tuna steaks, ¾in (2cm) thick
MARINADE:
1 small onion, finely chopped
4 scallions, finely chopped
2 cloves garlic, crushed
1in (2.5cm) piece fresh root ginger, grated
½ teaspoon hot pepper sauce
salt
CUCUMBER SALAD:
1 cucumber, peeled, deseeded, and chopped
1 teaspoon salt
1 clove garlic, crushed
1 tablespoon lime juice
1 small, fresh red chili, deseeded and finely chopped

To make marinade, in a shallow dish, mix together onion, scallions, garlic, ginger, hot pepper sauce, and salt to taste. Place tuna steaks in dish, and spoon the marinade over to coat. Cover and refrigerate for 2 hours.

To make cucumber salad, mix cucumber and salt together, and place in a colander for 10 minutes. Pat dry with paper towels. In a bowl, mix together cucumber, lime juice, and chili. Preheat broiler. Broil tuna for 5-7 minutes on each side and serve with cucumber salad.

Serves 4

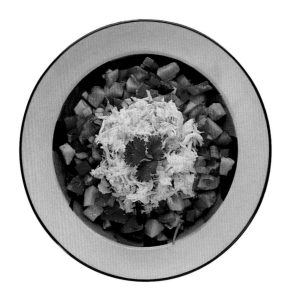

CRAB & PAPAYA SALAD

2 papayas, quartered
4 tomatoes
1 red onion, finely chopped
1 small red capsicum, finely diced
juice of ½ lemon
salt and freshly ground black pepper
½ red chili, deseeded and finely diced
¾in (2cm) piece fresh root ginger, finely chopped
1 tablespoon chopped fresh cilantro
1lb (450g) white crabmeat
GARNISH:
cilantro sprigs
cayenne pepper

Deseed the papaya quarters, peel and cut the flesh into small cubes. Place in a large bowl.

Place tomatoes in a bowl and cover with boiling water. Leave for 30 seconds then place in cold water for 30 seconds. Peel, cut into quarters, and remove seeds. Cut into dice, and add tomato and onion to the bowl with the papaya. Add capsicum.

Stir in lemon juice, seasoning, chili, ginger, and cilantro, and mix gently together. Leave to stand for 1 hour. Arrange papaya salad on 4 individual plates and pile crabmeat on top. Garnish with cilantro sprigs, and sprinkle with cayenne pepper.

Serves 4

CARIBBEAN SWORDFISH STEAKS

3 tablespoons oil
6 shallots, finely chopped
1 clove garlic, crushed
1 fresh green chili, deseeded and finely chopped
14oz (400g) can chopped tomatoes
2 bay leaves
¼ teaspoon cayenne pepper
1 teaspoon crushed allspice berries
juice of 2 limes
salt
4 swordfish steaks
1 teaspoon brown sugar
2 teaspoons Angostura bitters

Heat oil in a skillet. Add shallots and cook for 10 minutes until soft.

Add crushed garlic and chili, and cook for 2 minutes, then stir in tomatoes, bay leaves, cayenne pepper, allspice, lime juice, and salt. Cook gently for 15 minutes.

Add swordfish steaks to pan and baste with tomato sauce. Cover and cook for 10 minutes until steaks are cooked. Transfer swordfish steaks to a warmed dish and keep hot. Stir sugar and Angostura bitters into sauce. Simmer for 2 minutes, remove and discard bay leaves if liked, then serve sauce with fish.

Serves 4

PRAWN KABOBS & MANGO SALSA

1 fresh red chili, deseeded and finely chopped
½ teaspoon paprika
½ teaspoon ground coriander
1 clove garlic, crushed
juice of ½ lime
2 tablespoons oil
20 large, raw shrimp in shells, heads removed and
  deveined
MANGO SALSA:
1 mango, peeled and diced
½ small red onion, finely diced
1 fresh red chili, deseeded and finely chopped
3 tablespoons chopped fresh cilantro
grated rind and juice of 1 lime
salt and freshly ground black pepper

To make salsa, in a bowl mix together mango, red onion, chili, cilantro, lime rind and juice, and salt. Set aside.

In a bowl, mix together chili, paprika, coriander, garlic, lime juice, oil, and seasoning. Place shrimp in a dish. Add spice mixture and mix to coat thoroughly. Cover and leave in a cool place for 30 minutes. Preheat broiler. Thread shrimp on to skewers and broil, basting and turning frequently, for 6-8 minutes until pink. Serve with mango salsa.

Serves 4

CHICKEN PELAU

1 onion, roughly chopped
2 cloves garlic
2 celery sticks, roughly chopped
2 tablespoons chopped fresh chives
1 tablespoon fresh thyme leaves
liquid from 1 fresh coconut
½ fresh coconut, chopped
1 Scotch bonnet chili
2 tablespoons oil
2 tablespoons light soft brown sugar
3¾lb (1.75kg) chicken, cut into 2in (5cm) pieces
16oz (450g) can gungo peas, drained
1⅓ cups (8oz/225g) long-grain rice, washed
1⅓ cups (11fl oz/325ml) chicken stock
salt and freshly ground black pepper
12 pimento-stuffed olives, halved, to garnish

Place onion, garlic, celery, chives, and thyme in a blender or food processor with 4 tablespoons water and process to a paste. Transfer to a saucepan. Put coconut liquid and coconut in the blender or food processor, and blend until it will coat the back of a spoon. Add water if too thick. Stir into onion mixture with chili, and cook gently for 15 minutes.

Put oil and sugar in a wide-based, flameproof casserole. Heat gently until sugar begins to caramelize. Add chicken pieces and cook for 20 minutes, turning frequently, until well browned. Stir in coconut mixture, gungo peas, rice, and stock. Season and bring to the boil; cover and simmer for 20 minutes until chicken is tender, rice is cooked, and liquid has been absorbed. Remove and discard chili. Garnish with halved pimento-stuffed olives.

Serves 6

-CORNISH GAME HEN FRICASSEE-

2 cloves garlic, crushed
1 teaspoon paprika
1 teaspoon ground ginger
salt and freshly ground black pepper
2 Cornish game hens, quartered
2 tablespoons oil
1 large onion, coarsely chopped
8 scallions
3 tomatoes, peeled and chopped
1 Scotch bonnet chili
1 fresh bay leaf
chicken stock, if required
chopped fresh parsley, to garnish

In a bowl, mix together garlic, paprika, ginger, and seasoning. Rub over Cornish game hen portions and place in a dish. Cover and chill overnight. Scrape off and reserve marinade. Pat Cornish game hen portions dry with paper towels. Heat oil in a large, heavy skillet and fry Cornish game hen pieces, in batches, until golden all over. Transfer to a casserole. Add onion to skillet and cook for 10 minutes until soft.

Transfer to casserole and add scallions, tomatoes, chili, bay leaf, and reserved marinade. Cover and simmer gently for 30-40 minutes until Cornish game hen is thoroughly cooked. Add a little chicken stock if necessary, although there should not be a large quantity of liquid. Remove and discard chili and bay leaf. Serve garnished with chopped parsley.

Serves 4

DUCK WITH PINEAPPLE

4 duck breasts
salt and freshly ground black pepper
⅔ cup (5fl oz/150ml) dark rum
⅔ cup (5fl oz/150ml) unsweetened pineapple juice
1 pineapple
1¼ cups (10fl oz/300ml) chicken stock
2 teaspoons arrowroot

Season duck breasts. Heat a large, heavy-based skillet then place duck breasts, skin side down, in pan. Cook for a few minutes until skin is well browned and crisp. Turn over and brown underside. Pour off any fat.

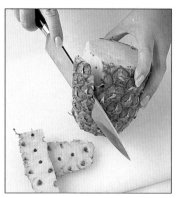

Pour 6 tablespoons of rum and 6 tablespoons of pineapple juice into pan. Allow to bubble up then cover pan and cook for 20-30 minutes until duck is cooked. Meanwhile, cut top off pineapple and reserve leaves for garnish, if you like. Cut away skin then cut pineapple into quarters lengthwise. Cut out core and discard. Chop pineapple flesh and reserve.

Add remaining rum to skillet, scraping any residue from base of pan. Pour into a saucepan and add remaining pineapple juice, and the stock. Boil until reduced to 1¾ cups (14fl oz/400ml). Season and stir in chopped pineapple. Mix arrowroot with a little cold water and stir into sauce. Cook, stirring, for a few minutes until slightly thickened. Slice duck breasts and fan out on 4 warmed plates. Garnish with pineapple leaves, if using, and serve with sauce.

Serves 4

CHICKEN WINGS WITH COLESLAW

½ cup (4fl oz/115ml) soy sauce
¼ cup (2fl oz/50ml) tomato catsup
¼ cup (2fl oz/50ml) white wine vinegar
¼ cup (2fl oz/50ml) clear honey
1 clove garlic, crushed
1 teaspoon ground ginger
pinch chili powder
12 chicken wings
COLESLAW:
4oz (115g) red cabbage, finely shredded
4oz (115g) white cabbage, finely shredded
1 carrot, grated
1 tablespoon chopped fresh parsley
2 teaspoons chopped fresh dill
4 tablespoons olive oil
1 tablespoon soy sauce

Put soy sauce, tomato catsup, vinegar, honey, garlic, ginger, and chili powder in an ovenproof dish and mix well. Add chicken wings and turn to coat thoroughly. Cover and chill overnight. To make coleslaw, place red cabbage, white cabbage, carrot, parsley, dill, olive oil, and soy sauce in a bowl and mix together. Set aside.

Preheat oven to 350F (180C). Bake dish of chicken wings for 30 minutes, turning after 15 minutes. Preheat broiler to medium. Place wings on a broiler pan and reserve marinade. Broil for 5-10 minutes, turning occasionally and brushing with reserved marinade, until brown and crisp. Serve with coleslaw.

Serves 4

NOTE: These chicken wings are ideal for cooking on a barbecue.

CALYPSO RABBIT

juice of 1 lime
salt and freshly ground black pepper
½ teaspoon chopped fresh thyme
2 cloves garlic, crushed
6 boneless rabbit portions
3 tablespoons oil
2 teaspoons brown sugar
1 cup (4oz/115g) cashew nuts
2 large onions, chopped
4oz (115g) mushrooms, sliced
1in (2.5cm) piece fresh root ginger, grated
¼ cup (2fl oz/50ml) chicken stock
few drops Angostura bitters
2 teaspoons arrowroot
thyme sprigs and lime slices, to garnish

In a dish, mix together lime juice, seasoning, thyme, and 1 clove garlic. Add rabbit pieces, and turn in marinade to coat thoroughly. Cover and leave in a cool place for 3 hours. In a flameproof casserole, heat half the oil. Add sugar and cook gently until bubbling. Add rabbit and fry, turning until evenly browned. Meanwhile, in a skillet, heat remaining oil. Add cashew nuts and cook gently until lightly browned. Remove nuts with a slotted spoon and set aside.

Add onions to pan and cook for 5 minutes. Stir in remaining garlic, the mushrooms, and ginger, and cook for 5 minutes. Stir in stock and Angostura bitters, and pour over rabbit. Stir in half the cashew nuts. Cover casserole and simmer gently for 30-40 minutes until rabbit is cooked through. In a bowl, mix arrowroot with a little water. Stir into rabbit mixture and simmer for 3 minutes. Scatter remaining cashew nuts over and garnish with thyme and lime slices. Serve with rice.

Serves 6

— CARIBBEAN CHICKEN SALAD —

4 chicken breast fillets with skin
salt and freshly ground black pepper
4 teaspoons jerk seasoning
1lb (450g) sweet potatoes, cut into chunks
½ cup (4fl oz/115ml) mayonnaise
2 tablespoons wholegrain mustard
2 tablespoons oil
1 onion, sliced
4oz (115g) button mushrooms
8oz (225g) small spinach leaves
3 tablespoons chopped fresh chives
lime juice, to taste

Preheat broiler. Season chicken with salt and jerk seasoning. Broil breasts for about 8 minutes on each side until cooked through. Set aside.

Place sweet potatoes in a pan of salted water. Bring to the boil and simmer for 5-8 minutes until tender, but not too soft. Drain and leave to cool. In a bowl, mix together mayonnaise and mustard. Add sweet potatoes and stir together. Set aside.

Heat oil in a large skillet. Add onion and cook for 10 minutes until soft and lightly browned. Add mushrooms and cook for 3 minutes. Season and add to sweet potato mixture with spinach and chives. Mix gently and add lime juice to taste. Cut chicken into thick diagonal slices and serve with salad.

Serves 4

MANGO TURKEY

1 clove garlic, crushed
1 teaspoon dried oregano
½ teaspoon ground allspice
salt and freshly ground black pepper
4 turkey steaks
7oz (200g) canned mango slices with their syrup
7oz (200g) can chopped tomatoes
1-2 teaspoons hot pepper sauce
1 tablespoon oil
1 tablespoon (½ oz/15g) butter
1 small mango, peeled and sliced, to garnish

In a dish, mix together garlic, oregano, all-spice and seasoning. Turn turkey steaks in mixture to coat. Cover and leave in a cool place for 1 hour.

Meanwhile, place canned mango slices with their syrup, and the tomatoes, in a blender or food processor and blend until smooth. Pour into a saucepan, and add hot pepper sauce and seasoning. Bring to the boil, cover, and simmer gently for 3 minutes. The sauce should be quite thick, but, if necessary, add a little water.

Heat oil and butter in a large skillet, and fry turkey steaks for about 5 minutes on each side until cooked through. Pour mango sauce into pan and simmer for 3 minutes. Meanwhile, preheat broiler. Broil fresh mango slices until lightly browned. Serve turkey with mango sauce, garnished with broiled mango slices. Serve with mashed sweet potatoes.

Serves 4

- QUAIL IN RUM & RAISIN SAUCE -

4 tablespoons dark rum
4 tablespoons raisins
1 tablespoon oil
8 quails
1 onion, sliced
1 clove garlic, sliced
1 teaspoon molasses
⅔ cup (5fl oz/150ml) chicken stock
1 teaspoon hot pepper sauce
salt and freshly ground black pepper
2 teaspoons arrowroot
chopped fresh cilantro, to garnish

Put rum and raisins in a bowl and leave to soak for 2 hours.

Heat oil in a flameproof casserole. Add quails and cook, turning frequently, until evenly browned. Remove and set aside. Add onion and garlic to casserole, and cook for 10 minutes until soft. Strain rum from raisins and put in a ladle or small saucepan. Heat gently then set alight with a taper and pour into casserole.

When flames die down, stir in molasses, stock, hot pepper sauce, and seasoning. Return quails to casserole. Cover and cook for 20-30 minutes until cooked through. Remove to a serving dish and keep warm. In a bowl, mix arrowroot with a little water and stir into sauce in casserole. Cook, stirring, for a few minutes until thickened. Pour over quails. Garnish with chopped cilantro and serve.

Serves 4

-SUGARED CHICKEN CASSEROLE-

8 chicken thighs
3 tablespoons oil
2 teaspoons superfine sugar
1 onion, finely chopped
2 sticks celery, chopped
½ cup (4fl oz/115ml) chicken stock
2 large plum tomatoes, deseeded and chopped
8oz (225g) okra
MARINADE:
1 red onion, roughly chopped
2 cloves garlic, roughly chopped
1in (2.5cm) piece fresh root ginger, chopped
1 red chili, deseeded and roughly chopped
2 tablespoons chopped fresh cilantro
1 tablespoon olive oil
juice of ½ lime
salt and freshly ground black pepper

To make marinade, put onion, garlic, ginger, chili, cilantro, olive oil, lime juice, and seasoning in a blender or food processor and process to a paste. Rub over chicken thighs and place in a dish. Cover and refrigerate overnight. Scrape marinade off chicken and reserve. Dry chicken thighs on paper towels. In a skillet, heat oil. Add sugar and cook gently until sugar dissolves. Add chicken and cook, turning frequently, until well browned.

Transfer to a casserole. Add onion and celery to oil in skillet and cook for 10 minutes until soft. Stir chicken stock into pan, scraping up any sediment, then pour over chicken. Bring to the boil then cover and simmer gently for 20 minutes. Add tomatoes and okra, and cook for a further 15 minutes. Add 2-3 tablespoons of reserved marinade, according to taste. Season and serve.

Serves 4

— BANANA-STUFFED CHICKEN —

3¾lb (1.75kg) chicken
1 tablespoon clear honey
juice of 1 small orange
½ cup (4fl oz/115ml) chicken stock
4 tablespoons rum
slices of orange, to garnish
STUFFING:
½ cup (3oz/85g) long-grain rice, cooked
3 bananas, mashed
grated rind and juice of 1 orange
¼ teaspoon cayenne pepper
¼ teaspoon freshly grated nutmeg
1 tablespoon rum
salt and freshly ground black pepper

Preheat oven to 350F (180C). To make stuffing, in a bowl mix together rice, bananas, orange rind and juice, cayenne pepper, nutmeg, rum, and seasoning. Fill chicken cavity with stuffing. Season chicken skin and place in a roasting pan. In a bowl, mix together honey and orange juice, and pour over chicken. Roast for 1½ hours, basting every 15 minutes, until chicken is brown and cooked through.

Transfer chicken to a heated serving dish and keep warm. Remove any fat from roasting pan and add stock and 1 tablespoon rum. Set over a high heat and cook, stirring and scraping up sediment, for a few minutes until slightly reduced. Just before serving, heat remaining rum, pour over chicken, and set alight with a taper. Garnish chicken with orange slices and serve with sauce.

Serves 6

—— CARIBBEAN LAMB CURRY ——

1¼lb (800g) trimmed shoulder of lamb, cut into 1in
  (2.5cm) cubes
finely grated rind and juice of 1 lime
3 cloves garlic, crushed
3 tablespoons oil
1 large onion, chopped
2 teaspoons medium curry powder
1 teaspoon ground cumin
1 tablespoon hot pepper sauce
2 teaspoons molasses
2 tablespoons tomato paste
2oz (50g) creamed coconut
salt
1 tablespoon chopped fresh cilantro

Place lamb in a bowl with lime rind and
juice, and garlic. Mix well, cover, and leave
in a cool place for 2 hours. In a flameproof
casserole, heat oil. Add onion and cook for
10 minutes until soft. Remove and set aside.
Drain meat (reserve any marinade) and pat
dry with paper towels. Add meat to hot oil,
in batches, and fry until well browned.
Return onions and browned meat to
casserole.

Stir in curry powder and cumin, and cook
for a further minute. Add hot pepper sauce,
molasses, tomato paste, and creamed
coconut, and cook for a further 5 minutes.
Add salt and about ⅔ cup (5fl oz/150ml)
water, to just cover meat. Bring to the boil
then reduce heat, cover, and simmer gently,
stirring occasionally, for 1½-2 hours until
meat is tender. Stir in cilantro. Serve with
cooked rice or Journey Cakes (see page 74).

Serves 4

JAMAICA PATTIES

1 tablespoon oil
1 red onion, finely chopped
1 clove garlic, crushed
9oz (250g) ground lamb or beef
1 green chili, finely chopped
2 large tomatoes, peeled and chopped
1-2 teaspoons medium curry powder
salt and freshly ground black pepper
beaten egg, for glazing
PASTRY:
3 cups (12oz/350g) all-purpose flour
1 teaspoon ground turmeric
¼ cup (6oz/175g) butter or hard margarine

Heat oil in a skillet, add onion and garlic, and cook for 10 minutes until soft. Add lamb or beef and stir until browned. Add chili, tomatoes, curry powder, and seasoning. Stir in ½ cup (4fl oz/115ml) water and simmer gently, stirring frequently, for 15-20 minutes until liquid has evaporated. Leave to cool.

To make pastry, sift flour, turmeric, and salt into a bowl. Rub in butter or margarine to resemble bread crumbs. Add about 3 table-spoons water to make a firm dough. Cover and chill for 1 hour. Preheat oven to 400F (200C). Divide pastry into 8 and roll into 7in (18cm) circles; place a spoonful of filling on one half of each. Moisten edges with water, fold pastry over, and press together firmly. Place on a baking sheet. Brush with egg and bake for 30 minutes until golden.

Makes 8

JERK PORK

1 tablespoon oil
2 onions, finely chopped
2 fresh red chilies, deseeded and finely chopped
1 clove garlic, crushed
1in (2.5cm) piece fresh root ginger, grated
1 teaspoon dried thyme
1 teaspoon ground allspice
1 teaspoon ground cinnamon
1 teaspoon hot pepper sauce
juice of 1 large orange
grated rind and juice of 1 lime
2 teaspoons brown sugar
salt and freshly ground black pepper
4 pork steaks or chops

In a skillet, heat oil. Add onions, and cook for 10 minutes until soft. Add chilies, garlic, ginger, thyme, allspice, and cinnamon, and fry for 2 minutes. Stir in hot pepper sauce, orange juice, lime rind and juice, and sugar. Simmer until mixture forms a dark paste. Season and leave to cool.

Rub paste over pork. Cover and chill overnight. Preheat oven to 375F (190C). Place pork on a rack in a roasting pan and roast for 30 minutes until cooked through.

Serves 4

STUFFED BAKED PAPAYA

1 green papaya, weighing about 4½lb (2kg)
2 tablespoons oil
1 onion, finely chopped
1 clove garlic, crushed
1lb (450g) lean ground pork
3 tomatoes, peeled and chopped
1 fresh green chili, deseeded and finely chopped
¼ teaspoon dried thyme
¼ teaspoon ground allspice
salt and freshly ground black pepper
4 tablespoons grated cheese
1 tablespoon fresh bread crumbs
lime wedges, to garnish

Preheat oven to 350F (180C). Cut papaya in half lengthwise and remove the seeds (peel the papaya if you prefer). Place papaya halves in a pan of boiling salted water and simmer for 10 minutes. Remove, drain thoroughly, and pat dry with paper towels. Place in a baking dish. Meanwhile, in a saucepan, heat oil. Add onion and garlic, and cook for 10 minutes until soft. Add pork and stir until browned.

Add tomatoes, chili, thyme, allspice, and seasoning and cook, stirring several times, for 15-20 minutes until thickened. Stir in half the cheese. Fill papaya halves with meat mixture. Mix together bread crumbs and remaining cheese and sprinkle on top. Bake for 30-40 minutes until browned on top and the papaya is tender. Garnish with lime slices and serve with tomato sauce if liked.

Serves 6

——— PINEAPPLE & GINGER RIBS ———

2lb (900g) pork spare ribs
4 tablespoons wine vinegar
MARINADE:
14oz (400g) can pineapple pieces in natural juice
2 tablespoons soy sauce
1 teaspoon hot pepper sauce
2in (5cm) piece fresh root ginger, grated
2 cloves garlic, crushed
2 tablespoons dark brown sugar
grated rind and juice of ½ lime
salt and freshly ground black pepper

Place spare ribs and vinegar in a large saucepan. Cover with water and bring slowly to the boil. Simmer for 15 minutes, then drain and cool.

To make marinade, in a blender or food processor, process pineapple pieces and juice until well blended. Add soy sauce, hot pepper sauce, ginger, garlic, sugar, lime rind and juice, and seasoning. Process to combine. Place ribs in a large roasting pan. Spoon marinade over and leave in a cool place for 2 hours.

Preheat oven to 350F (180C). Cover roasting pan with foil and bake ribs for 30 minutes. Turn oven up to 400F (200C). Remove foil and bake for a further 30 minutes until the ribs are well browned, sticky, and tender.

Serves 4

JAMAICAN PEPPERPOT

2 tablespoons oil
2 onions, chopped
2 cloves garlic, crushed
1¼lb (575g) shin of beef, cut into cubes
2½ cups (20fl oz/550ml) beef stock
9oz (250g) fresh spinach
1 teaspoon dried thyme
2 fresh green chilies, deseeded and chopped
8oz (225g) each sweet potato and pumpkin, cubed
1 green capsicum, chopped
2 tomatoes, peeled and chopped
salt and 2 teaspoons hot pepper sauce
DUMPLINGS:
2 cups (8oz/225g) all-purpose flour
1 tablespoon baking powder
2 tablespoons (1oz/25g) butter

In a flameproof casserole, heat oil. Add onions and garlic, and cook for 10 minutes until soft. Remove and set aside. Add beef to hot oil and fry in batches, until browned. Return onions and browned meat to casserole. Add stock, cover, and simmer gently for 1½ hours. Cook spinach in a little water then drain thoroughly and process in a food processor. Add to casserole with thyme, chilies, sweet potato, pumpkin, green capsicum, tomatoes, salt, and hot pepper sauce. Cook for a further 30 minutes until beef and vegetables are tender.

Meanwhile, make dumplings: sift flour, baking powder, and a little salt into a bowl. Rub in butter, and add enough cold water to make a dough. Shape into balls about 1½in (4cm) in diameter and flatten slightly. Drop into very gently simmering casserole about 10 minutes before end of cooking time.

Serves 4-6

──PORK & BANANA KABOBS──

1¼lb (575g) lean pork, cut into 1½in (4cm) cubes
3 bananas
12 slices bacon
1 red and 1 green capsicum, cut into 1½in (4cm)
  pieces
1 small pineapple, cubed
MARINADE:
1 teaspoon honey
1 teaspoon soy sauce
2 cloves garlic, crushed
4 tablespoons pineapple juice
1 tablespoon hot pepper sauce

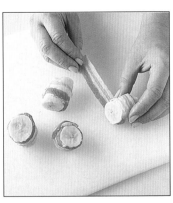

To make marinade, in a bowl, mix together honey, soy sauce, garlic, pineapple juice, and hot pepper sauce. Place pork in a dish and pour marinade over. Cover and leave in a cool place for at least 2 hours, turning occasionally. Cut each banana into 4 equal lengths. Roll each piece in a slice of bacon.

Preheat broiler. Thread 6 skewers with alternate pieces of red capsicum, pork, green capsicum, pork, pineapple, banana, and so on. Place skewers in a foil-lined broiler pan and cook for 10-15 minutes, turning occasionally and brushing with marinade, until pork is cooked through. Serve with rice.

Serves 6

—— PIONONOS & PLANTAIN ——

3 ripe plantains, peeled
2 eggs, beaten
oil, for frying
FILLING:
1 tablespoon oil
1 onion, finely chopped
1 clove garlic, crushed
1lb (450g) lean ground beef
2oz (50g) ham, ground
2 tomatoes, peeled and chopped
1 small green capsicum, finely chopped
1 tablespoon chopped fresh oregano
salt and freshly ground black pepper
juice of ½ lime
1 tablespoon capers, chopped
8 pimento-stuffed olives, chopped

Cut each plantain into 4 slices lengthwise. In a skillet, heat 2 tablespoons oil. Cook a few plantain slices at a time for 4 minutes, turning once, until browned. Drain on paper towels. When cool enough to handle, bend each slice into a circle and secure with a wooden toothpick. Set aside. To make filling, heat oil in pan. Add onion and garlic, and cook for 10 minutes. Add beef and stir until browned. Add ham, tomatoes, green capsicum, oregano, seasoning, and lime juice. Cook for 10-15 minutes, stirring frequently until thick. Stir in capers and olives.

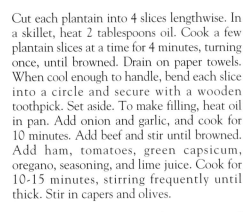

Fill each plantain ring with mixture and brush beaten egg over plantain rings, coating all sides. In a deep skillet, heat enough oil to come half way up plantain rings. Fry in batches for 2-3 minutes each side, turning gently, until golden brown. Drain on paper towels before serving with Rice and Peas (see page 61).

Serves 6

CARIBBEAN MEATBALLS

3 tablespoons oil
1 onion, finely chopped
1lb (450g) lean ground pork
1 cup (2oz/50g) fresh bread crumbs
1 egg, beaten
¼-½ teaspoon chili powder
1 teaspoon ground coriander
salt and freshly ground black pepper
TOMATO SAUCE:
2 tablespoons oil
1 onion, finely chopped
1 clove garlic, crushed
3 celery sticks, chopped
14oz (400g) can chopped tomatoes
1 teaspoon molasses
chopped fresh cilantro, to garnish

In a saucepan, heat half the oil. Add onion and cook for 10 minutes until soft. Set aside to cool. In a bowl, mix together onion, pork, bread crumbs, egg, chili powder, coriander, and seasoning until thoroughly combined. Divide mixture into 24 and form into balls. Set aside.

To make sauce, in a saucepan heat oil. Add onion, garlic, and celery, and cook for 10 minutes until soft. Add tomatoes, molasses, and seasoning. Bring to the boil, cover, and simmer for 15 minutes. Meanwhile, in a skillet, heat remaining oil. Fry meatballs, in batches if necessary, until brown on all sides. With a slotted spoon, transfer meatballs to the sauce. Simmer gently for 20 minutes. Serve garnished with chopped cilantro.

Serves 4-6

PICADILLO

2 tablespoons oil
2 onions, finely chopped
2 cloves garlic, crushed
1 green capsicum, chopped
1 red capsicum, chopped
1 green chili, finely chopped
1½lb (700g) ground beef
1lb (450g) tomatoes, peeled and chopped
½ teaspoon cumin seeds
2 teaspoons dried oregano
2 tablespoons raisins
salt and freshly ground black pepper
1½oz (40g) pimento-stuffed olives, sliced
1 tablespoon capers
rings of green and red capsicums, to garnish

In a large, heavy-based skillet, heat oil. Add onions, garlic, green and red capsicums, and chili, and cook for 10 minutes until soft Add beef and cook, stirring, until browned.

Add tomatoes, cumin, oregano, raisins, and seasoning, and simmer gently, uncovered, stirring frequently, for 20 minutes until meat is cooked and mixture is well blended. Add olives and capers, and cook for 5 minutes. Transfer to a heated serving dish and garnish with capsicum rings.

Serves 6

Note: Picadillo is traditionally served, topped with a fried egg and fried plantains, with black beans and rice.

— FRIED PLANTAIN & SPINACH —

1 large plantain
1 tablespoon (½oz/15g) butter
1 tablespoon oil
4 scallions, roughly chopped
8oz (225g) small spinach leaves
freshly grated nutmeg, to taste
salt and freshly ground black pepper
fresh red chili slices, to garnish

Cut ends off plantain. Slit skin lengthwise in several places, then peel off the strips of skin. Cut plantain into cubes.

In a skillet, heat butter and oil. Add plantain cubes and fry for 3-4 minutes, turning frequently, until golden brown and cooked. Add scallions and cook for 1 more minute.

Add spinach and cook for 1 minute until just wilted. Sprinkle with nutmeg and seasoning. Garnish with slices of red chili.

Serves 4

GREEN BANANA CURRY

5 green bananas
2 tablespoons oil
1 onion, finely sliced
1 tablespoon curry paste
14fl oz (400ml) can coconut milk
salt and freshly ground black pepper
GARNISH:
chopped fresh cilantro
lime wedges

Slice skin off bananas and cut flesh into 1in (2.5cm) slices. Heat oil in a deep skillet and fry banana slices, in batches, until lightly browned on each side. Set aside. Add onion to pan and cook for 10 minutes until soft. Return banana slices to pan and stir in curry paste.

Add half the coconut milk and stir well. Cook for 10 minutes over a low heat then add seasoning. Pour in remaining coconut milk, and simmer until mixture thickens and the bananas break down a little. Garnish with cilantro and lime wedges, and serve immediately.

Serves 4

OKRA & TOMATOES

1lb (450g) fresh young okra
3 tablespoons olive oil
1 small onion, chopped
1 stick celery, chopped
1 red chili, finely chopped
1 clove garlic, crushed
1lb (450g) tomatoes, peeled and chopped
1 tablespoon lime juice
salt and freshly ground black pepper
1 teaspoon sugar
chopped fresh parsley, to garnish

Cut stalks off okra, taking care not to pierce pods. In a large skillet, heat oil. Add onion and celery, and cook gently for 10 minutes until soft. Add okra, chili, and garlic, and turn carefully in the oil. Cook for 5 minutes.

Add tomatoes, lime juice, seasoning, and sugar. Cover and simmer gently for 10 minutes. Remove the lid and cook for a further 10 minutes until okra are tender and the sauce reduced. If sauce becomes too dry, add a little water. Serve hot or cold, garnished with chopped parsley.

Serves 4-6

CURRIED POTATO ROTI

2¼ cups (9oz/250g) all-purpose flour
2 teaspoons baking powder
oil, for brushing
yogurt, to serve
POTATO CURRY FILLING:
2 tablespoons oil
1 small onion, finely chopped
1 clove garlic, thinly sliced
1 tablespoon curry powder
1lb (450g) potatoes, cut into small cubes
salt

To make filling, in a saucepan, heat oil. Add onion and garlic, and cook gently for 10 minutes until soft. Add curry powder and stir for 2-3 minutes. Add potatoes, salt, and ⅔ cup (5fl oz/150ml) water. Cover and simmer gently for 10-15 minutes until tender and quite dry. Set aside. Sift flour, baking powder, and salt into a bowl. Stir in enough water to make a stiff dough. Knead until smooth. Divide dough into 8 and roll each piece into a 4in (10cm) circle. Brush with oil and roll into balls again. Cover and leave for 20 minutes.

Roll out dough balls into 6in (15cm) circles. Place a spoonful of filling in center of each circle. Fold edges over to enclose filling. Roll lightly on each side with a rolling pin. Brush with oil. Heat a heavy skillet and cook roti for 3 minutes on each side or until browned. Serve with yogurt.

Serves 4

GARBANZO CAKES & CHILI RELISH

2x15oz (425g) cans garbanzos, drained
2 cloves garlic, crushed
1 bunch scallions, chopped
2 teaspoons ground cumin
2 tablespoons chopped fresh cilantro
1 small egg, beaten
2 tablespoons all-purpose flour
salt and freshly ground black pepper
seasoned flour, for shaping
oil, for shallow frying
CHILI RELISH:
4 tomatoes, peeled and diced
2 fresh red chilies, deseeded and finely chopped
1 small red onion, finely chopped
juice of 1 lime
3 tablespoons chopped fresh cilantro

In a blender or food processor, process garbanzos until smooth. Add garlic, scallions, and cumin. Process again until well combined. Spoon into a bowl and stir in fresh cilantro, egg, flour, and seasoning. Mix well; if very soft, add a little more flour. Chill for about 30 minutes to firm up.

Meanwhile, make chili relish. In a bowl, mix together all ingredients and salt. Set aside. With floured hands, shape garbanzo mixture into 12 cakes. In a skillet, heat oil and fry cakes, in batches if necessary, for 2-3 minutes on each side, until crisp and golden. Drain on paper towels and serve with chili relish.

Serves 4

— CARIBBEAN RATATOUILLE —

2 tablespoons oil
1 large onion, thinly sliced
2 cloves garlic, crushed
1 red chili, deseeded and finely chopped
1 eggplant, peeled and cut into 1in (2.5cm) cubes
1 red capsicum, cut into cubes
1 green capsicum, cut into cubes
4oz (115g) okra, sliced
1 chayote, peeled, deseeded, and chopped
1lb (450g) tomatoes, peeled and roughly chopped
1 teaspoon sugar
1 teaspoon dried thyme
2 teaspoons chopped fresh basil
salt and freshly ground black pepper
fresh basil leaves, to garnish

Heat oil in a flameproof casserole. Add onion and cook for 10 minutes until soft. Stir in garlic and chili, and cook for 2 more minutes. Stir in eggplant, red and green capsicums, okra, chayote, tomatoes, sugar, thyme, basil, and seasoning.

Cover and cook gently for 20-30 minutes, stirring occasionally, until vegetables are almost cooked. Remove lid and simmer for a few minutes until vegetables are tender and most of the liquid has evaporated. Serve hot or cold, garnished with basil leaves.

Serves 6

VARIATION: The vegetables may be varied according to taste and what is available. Zucchini and celery may be used instead of chayote and okra.

—— ROAST SPICED PUMPKIN ——

1 small pumpkin or large butternut squash
1 teaspoon coriander seeds
2 teaspoons allspice berries
2 small dried chilies
1 teaspoon dried thyme
salt
½ teaspoon black peppercorns
1 clove garlic
1 tablespoon oil

Preheat oven to 400F (200C). Cut pumpkin or squash in half and remove seeds. Do not peel. Cut each half lengthwise into wedges about 1in (2.5cm) thick. In a mortar and pestle or spice grinder, grind together coriander seeds, allspice berries, chilies, thyme, salt, peppercorns, and garlic, to make a coarse powder.

Place pumpkin or squash slices in a roasting pan. Add spices and oil and toss pumpkin or squash in mixture to coat thoroughly. Roast for 30 minutes until pumpkin or squash is tender and lightly browned.

Serves 6

BEAN SALAD

1¼ cups (8oz/225g) red kidney beans, soaked
  overnight
sprig fresh thyme
4 sticks celery, chopped
1 green capsicum, chopped
1 small red onion, finely chopped
salad leaves, to serve
celery leaves, to garnish
DRESSING:
4 tablespoons olive oil
1 tablespoon lime juice
½-1 teaspoon hot pepper sauce
1 teaspoon sugar
1 tablespoon chopped fresh cilantro
salt

Drain beans and put in a large saucepan
with thyme sprig and plenty of cold water.
Bring to the boil and boil vigorously for
10 minutes. Reduce heat, cover pan and
simmer for 45-60 minutes until beans are
tender. Drain beans and remove and discard
thyme.

To make dressing, in a bowl whisk together
olive oil, lime juice, hot pepper sauce, sugar,
cilantro, and salt. Pour over warm beans,
mix together thoroughly and leave to cool.
Gently stir in celery, green capsicum, and
onion. Arrange salad leaves in a serving
bowl and pile beans on top. Garnish with
celery leaves.

Serves 4

YAM SALAD

1½lb (700g) yam
2 dill pickles, sliced
2 hard-cooked eggs, quartered
8 cherry tomatoes, halved
¼ cucumber, peeled and diced
4 scallions, sliced
1 fresh red chili, deseeded and finely chopped
1 tablespoon chopped fresh chives
DRESSING:
⅔ cup (5fl oz/150ml) mayonnaise
4 tablespoons crème fraîche
2 tablespoons lime juice
salt and freshly ground black pepper

To make dressing, in a bowl, mix together mayonnaise, crème fraîche, lime juice, and seasoning. Set aside. Place unpeeled yam in a saucepan. Cover with cold water, add salt, and bring to the boil. Cover and simmer for 25-30 minutes until tender. Drain. When cool enough to handle, peel yam and cut into cubes. Place yam cubes in a large bowl and pour dressing over. Mix well to coat and leave to cool.

Carefully stir in dill pickles, eggs, cherry tomatoes, cucumber, scallions, chili, chives, and seasoning. Transfer to a serving bowl, cover and chill for 1 hour.

Serves 6

RICE & PEAS

2 cups (12oz/350g) basmati rice, washed and soaked
   for 1 hour
16fl oz (450ml) can coconut milk
1 sprig fresh thyme
1 Scotch bonnet chili
salt and freshly ground black pepper
1 tablespoon oil
4 scallions, sliced
1 clove garlic, crushed
14oz (400g) can gungo peas, drained and rinsed

Drain rice and put in a saucepan with
coconut milk, thyme, chili, and salt. Bring
to the boil and stir once. Lower heat so
liquid simmers gently, cover with a tightly
fitting lid and cook for 10-12 minutes until
rice is tender and liquid is absorbed.

Meanwhile, heat oil in a large pan. Add
scallions and garlic and cook for 2-3
minutes. Remove thyme and chili from rice
and discard. Carefully stir scallion mixture,
gungo peas, and freshly ground black pepper
into rice and heat through gently.

Serves 6

JAMAICAN RICE SALAD

1⅓ cups (8oz/225g) long-grain rice
salt and freshly ground black pepper
1 red capsicum, halved
1 yellow capsicum, halved
1 fresh green chili, deseeded and finely chopped
¾ cup (3oz/85g) roasted, salted cashew nuts
flesh of ½ coconut, coarsely grated
⅓ cup (2oz/50g) seedless raisins
grated rind and juice of ½ orange
⅔ cup (5fl oz/150ml) mayonnaise
1 banana, sliced
chopped fresh chives, to garnish

In a pan of boiling salted water, cook rice for 10-15 minutes until tender. Drain then rinse under cold running water. Drain again and set aside. Preheat grill. Broil capsicums, skin side up, and cook until skins have blackened. Place in a plastic bag until cool enough to handle then peel off skins and cut flesh into strips.

In a bowl, stir together rice, capsicums, chili, cashew nuts, coconut, and raisins. In another bowl, mix orange rind and juice with mayonnaise. Stir mayonnaise into rice mixture, then carefully stir in banana. Transfer to a serving dish, scatter with chives, and serve immediately.

Serves 6

-VEGETABLE & COCONUT CURRY-

1 butternut squash, peeled, deseeded, and cubed
2 sweet potatoes, cubed
2 carrots, cubed
3 tablespoons oil
3 cloves garlic, crushed
1 large onion, chopped
1 fresh red chili, deseeded and finely chopped
1 teaspoon ground cumin
2 teaspoons medium curry powder
2 teaspoons molasses
2 tablespoons tomato paste
2oz (50g) creamed coconut
salt
⅔ cup (5fl oz/150ml) vegetable stock
finely grated rind and juice of 1 lime
1 tablespoon chopped fresh cilantro

Place squash, sweet potatoes, and carrots in a pan of salted water. Bring to the boil and simmer for 5-8 minutes until barely tender. Drain and set aside. In a flameproof casserole heat oil. Add garlic and onion, and cook for 10 minutes until soft. Stir in chili, cumin, and curry powder, and cook for a further minute.

Add molasses, tomato paste, and creamed coconut, and cook for 1 minute. Add salt, stock, lime rind and juice, and vegetables. Bring to the boil then reduce the heat, cover, and simmer gently, stirring occasionally, for 10-15 minutes until vegetables are soft. Stir in cilantro. Serve with rice.

Serves 4

- PALM HEART & PAPAYA SALAD -

2 ripe papayas
2 firm, ripe avocados
14oz (400g) can palm hearts, drained and sliced
lime rind, to garnish
DRESSING:
juice of 1 lime
1 teaspoon Dijon mustard
1 teaspoon hot pepper sauce
1 clove garlic, crushed
salt and freshly ground black pepper
4 tablespoons olive oil

To make the dressing, in a bowl whisk together lime juice, mustard, hot pepper sauce, garlic, seasoning, and olive oil. Set aside. Cut papayas in half and scoop out the seeds. Remove the skin and cut into 8 slices lengthwise.

Peel avocados, cut in half and discard pits. Slice lengthwise. Arrange palm hearts, and avocado and papaya slices on 6 plates and drizzle the dressing over. Garnish with lime rind and serve immediately.

Serves 6

CALLALOO GRATIN

butter, for greasing
1 tablespoon oil
1 large onion, chopped
1 clove garlic, crushed
20oz (575g) can callaloo, drained
scant 1 cup (3½oz/100g) Cheddar cheese, grated
2 eggs, beaten
½ teaspoon freshly grated nutmeg
salt and freshly ground black pepper
2 tablespoons fresh bread crumbs

Preheat oven to 350F (180C). Butter an ovenproof dish. Heat oil in a skillet. Add onion and garlic and cook for 10 minutes until soft. Add callaloo and cook until excess moisture has evaporated. Leave to cool. Set aside 2 tablespoons cheese and place remainder in a bowl with eggs, nutmeg, and seasoning. Mix together thoroughly.

Stir cooled callaloo mixture into bowl. Pour into prepared dish. Scatter reserved cheese and the bread crumbs on top. Bake for 45 minutes until firm and lightly browned.

Serves 4

———— GRENADAN COO-COO ————

14fl oz (400ml) can coconut milk
1¼ cups (8oz/225g) coarse cornmeal
oil, for shallow frying and/or brushing
PAPAYA SALSA:
1 papaya
½ small red onion, finely diced
1 fresh chili, deseeded and finely chopped
3 tablespoons chopped fresh cilantro
grated rind and juice of 1 lime
salt and freshly ground black pepper

To make salsa, cut papaya in half and scoop out the seeds. Remove the skin, cut the flesh into small dice and place in a bowl. Add onion, chili, cilantro, lime rind and juice and salt. Mix well and set aside. Pour coconut milk into a pan with 2 cups (16fl oz/450ml) water. Add seasoning. Bring to the boil and pour in cornmeal in a steady stream, stirring with a wooden spoon. Cook, stirring constantly, for about 5 minutes until the mixture is thick and smooth.

Turn on to a wooden board or large plate, to form a circle 8in (20cm) in diameter and leave until cold and firm. Preheat grill or heat a little oil in a skillet. Cut coo-coo into wedges, brush on both sides with oil, and grill or fry until browned. Serve with salsa.

Serves 6

VARIATIONS: Serve, without the salsa, with meat or fish dishes. It can be served immediately after cooking in the pan.

——— GLAZED SWEET POTATO ———

3 tablespoons (1½oz/40g) butter
3 tablespoons oil
2lb (1kg) sweet potatoes, cut into ½in (1cm) cubes
2 cloves garlic, crushed
2 pieces stem ginger, finely chopped
2 teaspoons ground allspice
2 teaspoons chopped fresh thyme
¼ teaspoon cayenne pepper
1 tablespoon syrup from the ginger jar
1 teaspoon brown sugar
salt
thyme sprigs, to garnish

In a skillet, heat butter and oil. Add sweet potato cubes and fry, stirring frequently, for about 10 minutes until just soft. Stir in garlic, ginger, and allspice. Cook, stirring, for 5 minutes.

Stir in thyme, cayenne pepper, ginger syrup, sugar, and salt. Stir for 1-2 minutes until browned and tender. Serve garnished with thyme sprigs.

Serves 4

CHILI CORNBREAD

1 cup (4oz/115gm) all-purpose flour
1 tablespoon baking powder
salt
½ teaspoon ground mace
⅔ cup (4oz/115g) cornmeal
2 eggs
1¼ cups (10fl oz/300ml) milk
¼ cup (2oz/50g) butter, melted
1 fresh red chili, deseeded and very finely chopped
1 fresh green chili, deseeded and very finely chopped
7oz (200g) can sweetcorn, drained

Preheat oven to 400F (200C). Grease and line a 2lb (900g) loaf pan. Sift flour, baking powder, salt, and mace into a large bowl. Stir in cornmeal. In a large jug, whisk together eggs, milk, and melted butter. Make a well in center of dry mixture and pour in liquid. Mix thoroughly until smooth.

Stir in red and green chilies, and sweetcorn. Pour into prepared loaf pan. Bake for 55-60 minutes until well risen, firm, and lightly browned. Leave in pan for 5 minutes then turn on to a wire rack to cool.

Serves 8

BANANA BREAD

½ cup (4oz/115g) butter
¾ cup (4oz/115g) brown sugar
2 egg, beaten
2 cups (8oz/225g) all-purpose flour
1 tablespoon baking powder
1 teaspoon ground allspice
½ teaspoon grated nutmeg
3 ripe bananas, mashed
¾ cup (4oz/115g) chopped dates
1 cup (4oz/115g) roughly chopped pecan nuts
dried banana slices, to decorate

Preheat oven to 350F (180C). Grease and line a 2lb (900g) loaf pan. In a bowl, beat together butter and sugar. Gradually beat in egg. Sift flour, baking powder, allspice, and nutmeg into another bowl. Stir sifted ingredients and the banana alternately into egg mixture, beating after each addition, until thoroughly blended.

Carefully stir in dates and pecan nuts. Spoon mixture into prepared pan. Place dried bananas lightly on top. Bake for about 1 hour until a skewer inserted into the center comes out clean. Leave in pan for 5 minutes then turn on to a wire rack to cool.

Serves 8

ORANGE SYRUP CAKE

5 oranges
½ cup (4oz/115g) softened butter
½ cup (4oz/115g) superfine sugar
2 eggs, beaten
1 cup (6oz/175g) semolina
scant 1 cup (3½oz/100g) ground almonds
1 teaspoon mixed spice
1½ teaspoons baking powder
ORANGE AND LIME SYRUP:
juice of 3 oranges
juice of 1 lime
½ cup (4oz/115g) superfine sugar
1 cinnamon stick, broken

Preheat oven to 350F (180C). Butter and base-line a 8in (20cm) round cake pan. Grate rind from 1 orange and squeeze juice from one half. In a bowl, beat together butter, orange rind, and sugar until light and creamy. Gradually beat in eggs. Mix together semolina, ground almonds, mixed spice, and baking powder and fold into creamed mixture with reserved orange juice. Spoon mixture into the prepared pan and bake for 30-40 minutes until well risen and a skewer inserted into the center comes out clean. Leave to cool in pan for a few minutes.

Meanwhile, peel and slice remaining oranges and set aside. To make syrup, in a pan, gently heat orange and lime juices, sugar, and cinnamon. When sugar has dissolved, bring to boil and simmer for 30 minutes until syrupy. Turn cake on to a deep serving dish. Using a skewer, make holes in warm cake. Spoon or pour ¾ of the syrup over and leave for 30 minutes. Place reserved orange slices in remaining syrup and leave to cool. Serve with cake.

Serves 8

– CARIBBEAN CHRISTMAS CAKE –

4½ cups (1½lb/700g) luxury dried mixed fruit
1¼ cups (8oz/225g) ready-to-eat prunes, chopped
1¼ cups (8oz/225g) ready-to-eat dried mango,
   chopped
⅓ cup (2oz/50g) candied cherries, quartered
3 cups (25fl oz/700ml) dark rum
1 cup (8oz/225g) butter, softened
1⅓ cups (9oz/250g) dark brown sugar
2 cups (8oz/225g) all-purpose flour
2 teaspoons baking powder
1 tablespoon mixed spice
6 eggs, beaten
4 tablespoons molasses
almond-paste fruits or candied fruits, to decorate

Put mixed fruit, prunes, mango, cherries, and 2½ cups (20fl oz/600ml) rum in a saucepan. Heat gently until beginning to boil, then reduce heat and simmer for 5 minutes. Cool then leave overnight. Preheat oven to 300F (150C). Grease and line a 9in (23cm) round pan and wrap a double layer of brown paper round outside. In a bowl, cream together butter and sugar until light and fluffy. Sift flour, baking powder, and spice into a bowl, then gradually add flour mixture to butter and sugar, alternating with eggs, beating well after each addition.

Stir in molasses then stir into soaked fruits. Spoon into prepared pan and smooth the top. Bake for 2½-3 hours until a skewer inserted into the center comes out clean. Prick cake all over with a fork and pour over remaining rum. When sizzling stops, cool cake in pan. Remove from pan and discard lining paper. Wrap in foil until needed. To serve, decorate with almond-paste or candied fruits.

Makes 9in (23cm) cake

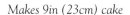

—— JAMAICAN GINGER CAKE ——

2 cups (8oz/225g) self-rising flour
1 tablespoon ground ginger
¼ teaspoon freshly ground nutmeg
½ teaspoon baking soda
½ cup (4oz/115g) butter
¾ cup (4oz/115g) dark brown sugar
2 eggs
1½ tablespoons corn syrup
1½ tablespoons milk
TOPPING:
6 pieces stem ginger, quartered
1 cup (4oz/115g) confectioners' sugar
4 teaspoons syrup from ginger jar
lemon juice

Preheat oven to 325F (170C). Grease and line an 7in (18cm) square cake pan. Sift flour, ginger, nutmeg, and baking soda into a bowl. Rub in butter then stir in sugar. Make a well in center. In a bowl, whisk together eggs, syrup, and milk. Pour into flour mixture, and beat until smooth and glossy. Spoon into prepared pan and bake for 45-50 minutes until well risen and firm to the touch. Leave in pan for 30 minutes, then remove to a wire rack to cool completely.

To make topping, arrange ginger pieces on top of cake. Sift confectioners' sugar into a bowl and stir in ginger syrup and enough lemon juice to make a smooth frosting. Put frosting into a baking-parchment piping bag and drizzle over top of cake. Leave to set. Store in an airtight container for 1 day before cutting into squares and serving.

Makes 12 squares

— PINEAPPLE & COCONUT CAKE —

1lb (450g) can pineapple in natural juice, drained
1¼ cups (5oz/150g) all-purpose flour
¾ cup (4oz/115g) dark brown sugar
½ cup (4oz/115g) butter, softened
2 eggs
2 teaspoons baking powder
1 teaspoon ground allspice
⅔ cup (2oz/50g) unsweetened flaked coconut
TO DECORATE:
unsweetened flaked coconut
confectioners' sugar

Preheat oven to 350F (180C). Cut pineapple into large chunks. Grease and base-line a 1lb (450g) loaf pan. Place flour and sugar in a food processor, and blend until thoroughly combined.

Add butter, eggs, baking powder, allspice, and coconut and process until smooth. Stir in pineapple. Turn into prepared pan. Level surface and brush lightly with a little cold water. Bake for 50 minutes until well risen and a skewer inserted into center comes out clean. If it browns too quickly, cover after 40 minutes. Leave in pan for 10 minutes then transfer to a wire rack to cool. Sprinkle with unsweetened flaked coconut and sift confectioners' sugar on top.

Serves 8

JOURNEY CAKES

2 cups (8oz/225g) all-purpose flour
2 teaspoons baking powder
salt
1 teaspoon superfine sugar
2 tablespoons (1oz/25g) butter
oil, for frying

Sift flour, baking powder, salt, and sugar into a large bowl.

Add butter, and rub in until mixture resembles fine bread crumbs. Alternatively, blend ingredients in a food processor. Add about ½ cup (4fl oz/115ml) cold water and mix to a stiffish dough. Divide into 8 pieces.

On an oiled board, flatten each piece slightly. Heat oil in a skillet and fry journey cakes, in batches, for 4-5 minutes on each side until golden brown. Drain on paper towels and serve hot with soup and stews.

Serves 4

NOTE: These little fried cakes are also known as Bakes or Johnny Cakes.

– CHEESE & CORNMEAL MUFFINS –

1 cup (4oz/115g) self-rising flour
1 tablespoon baking powder
¼ teaspoon cayenne pepper
salt
2 cups (8oz/225g) fine cornmeal
1¼ cups (5oz/150g) grated Cheddar cheese
¼ cup (2oz/50g) butter, melted
2 large eggs, beaten
1¼ cups (10fl oz/300ml) milk

Preheat oven to 400F (200C). Thoroughly grease 12 deep muffin cups or line cups with paper muffin cases. Sift flour, baking powder, cayenne pepper, and salt into a bowl, then stir in cornmeal and 1 cup (4oz/115g) grated cheese. Pour melted butter into a bowl and stir in eggs and milk. Pour on to dry ingredients and mix quickly until just combined. Do not overmix.

Spoon batter into prepared muffin cups. Scatter reserved cheese on top and bake for 20 minutes until golden brown. Leave to cool for a few minutes before transferring to a wire rack to cool.

Makes 12

— MANGO UPSIDE-DOWN CAKE —

1 cup (8oz/225g) butter
⅓ cup (2oz/50g) dark brown sugar
11oz (325g) can mango slices in syrup
1 cup (6oz/175g) light soft brown sugar
3 eggs, beaten
1½ cups (6oz/175g) self-rising flour, sifted
2 teaspoons ground ginger
1 teaspoon mixed spice

Preheat oven to 350F (180C). In a saucepan, melt ¼ cup (2oz/50g) butter. Stir in dark brown sugar. Spread over base of a 8-9in (20-23cm) cake pan.

Drain mangoes, reserving 3 tablespoons syrup. Arrange mangoes in pan. In a bowl, beat together remaining butter and the light brown sugar until light and fluffy. Gradually beat in eggs, adding 1 tablespoon flour towards the end. Fold in remaining flour, the ginger, mixed spice, and reserved mango syrup.

Spread mixture over mango and bake for 55-60 minutes until sponge springs back when lightly pressed. Leave in pan for 5 minutes then turn on to a serving dish. Serve warm or cold.

Serves 6-8

—— COCONUT ICE CREAM ——

2oz (50g) creamed coconut
2 eggs, separated
½ cup (4oz/115g) superfine sugar
1¼ cups (10fl oz/300ml) light cream
3 tablespoons coconut liqueur
⅔ cup (5fl oz/150ml) thick cream, whipped
pulp of 6 passion fruit, to serve

Set freezer to maximum. In a bowl, blend creamed coconut with 2 tablespoons hot water. Add egg yolks and half the sugar, and beat well.

In a saucepan, heat light cream. Bring to the boil then pour on to egg yolk mixture, stirring vigorously. Return to pan and cook gently until slightly thickened. Leave to cool. Stir in coconut liqueur. In another bowl, whisk egg whites until stiff, then whisk in remaining sugar. Fold into whipped cream then fold in coconut custard.

Pour mixture into a shallow freezerproof container. Cover and freeze for 3 hours until just frozen. Spoon into a bowl and mash with a fork or whisk to break down ice crystals. Return mixture to container and freeze again for 2 hours, mash once more then freeze for 2-3 hours until firm. Remove from freezer and leave at room temperature for 20-30 minutes before serving. Serve with passion fruit pulp.

Serves 6

—BANANA & GINGER ICE CREAM—

16fl oz (450ml) can evaporated milk, chilled
½ cup (4oz/115g) light brown sugar
3 ripe bananas, mashed
2 tablespoons syrup from ginger jar
4oz (115g) preserved stem ginger, chopped
ginger syrup, to serve

Turn freezer to its coldest setting. Pour evaporated milk into a bowl and, using an electric beater, whisk until thick and mousse-like. Whisk in sugar.

Whisk bananas and ginger syrup into evaporated milk. Stir in chopped ginger. Cover and freeze for 3 hours until just frozen. Spoon into a bowl and mash with a fork or whisk to break down ice crystals.

Return mixture to container and freeze again for 2 hours. Mash once more then freeze for 2-3 hours until firm. Remove from freezer and leave at room temperature for 20-30 minutes before serving. Scoop into chilled glasses, and serve with a little ginger syrup drizzled over.

Serves 6-8

— SPICED SWEET POTATO TART —

1lb 2oz (500g) sweet potatoes, diced
2 eggs, beaten
2 cups (16fl oz/450ml) evaporated milk
⅓ cup (3oz/85g) light brown sugar
1 tablespoon mixed spice
PASTRY:
1½ cups (6oz/175g) all-purpose flour
salt
⅓ cup (3oz/85g) butter
1 teaspoon superfine sugar
1 egg yolk

Cook sweet potatoes in boiling water for 10 minutes; drain thoroughly. Mash until smooth. Leave to cool. To make pastry, sift flour and salt into a bowl. Rub in butter to resemble bread crumbs. Add sugar. Mix in egg yolk and enough cold water to make a firm dough. On a floured surface, roll out pastry and use to line a 9in (23cm) round quiche pan. Chill for 30 minutes. Preheat oven to 375F (190C). Line pastry shell with baking parchment and baking beans. Bake for 10 minutes. Remove paper and beans and return to oven for 5 minutes.

In a large bowl, mix together sweet potato, eggs, evaporated milk, sugar, and mixed spice. Pour into pie shell and bake for 30 minutes. Reduce heat to 350F (180C) and bake for a further 10-15 minutes until filling is set. Serve hot or cold, dusted with confectioners' sugar, if you like.

Serves 8

—— PINEAPPLE TART TATIN ——

10oz (300g) puff pastry
½ cup (4oz/115g) butter
½ cup (4oz/115g) granulated sugar
4 tablespoons heavy cream
2 small-medium pineapples, total weight about 2lb
  (1kg), thinly sliced, cores removed

Preheat oven to 425F (220C). On a floured surface, roll out pastry to a circle slightly larger than a 8½in (22cm) non-stick shallow cake pan. Transfer to a baking sheet, prick pastry lightly and chill.

In a small pan, gently heat butter and sugar until melted. Bring to the boil then simmer for 3-4 minutes, beating continuously until smooth, dark and fudge-like. Remove from heat, cool for 1 minute then beat in cream. If necessary, warm slightly then spoon into pan. Arrange overlapping circles of pineapple slices in cake pan.

Bake for 20-25 minutes until pastry is well risen and golden. Run a knife round the edge of pastry to loosen, then leave in pan for 2-3 minutes until juices stop bubbling. Invert on to a heatproof serving dish. Place under a hot broiler for 2-3 minutes to caramelize the top. Serve warm with crème fraîche sprinkled with a little nutmeg, if you like.

Serves 6

— FLAMBEED TROPICAL FRUIT —

1 small pineapple, peeled, cored, and chopped
coarsely ground black pepper
1 teaspoon ground cinnamon
grated rind and juice of ½ orange
2 tablespoons light soft brown sugar
3 tablespoons (1½oz/40g) butter
1 large ripe mango, peeled and chopped
2 bananas, sliced
2 tablespoons rum

Put pineapple in a bowl. Season with pepper. Stir in cinnamon and orange rind. In a skillet, heat sugar and butter until melted. Add pineapple and orange juice and cook for 3 minutes until beginning to soften.

Add mango and bananas to skillet. Pour rum into a ladle or small pan, warm over a flame and ignite. Pour over fruit. When flames have died down, divide the fruit between four plates. Decorate with pineapple leaves, if you like.

Serves 4

—— BANANA & RUM BRULEE ——

scant 1 cup (7fl oz/200ml) coconut cream
1¾ cups (14fl oz/400ml) heavy cream
1 vanilla pod, split
6 egg yolks
½ cup (4oz/115g) superfine sugar
2 small bananas, sliced
4 tablespoons dark rum
6 tablespoons brown sugar
mint leaves, to decorate

Preheat oven to 325F (170C). Put coconut cream, cream, and vanilla pod in a saucepan and heat gently until almost boiling. Do not boil. In a bowl, whisk together egg yolks and superfine sugar until creamy. Strain in hot cream. Place bowl over a saucepan of simmering water. Stir continuously until custard is thick enough to coat the back of a spoon. In a bowl, toss together banana and rum. Divide among 6 ramekin dishes. Pour custard over.

Place dishes in a roasting pan and pour in hot water to come half-way up sides of ramekins. Bake for 5 minutes to create a skin on top. Allow to cool then refrigerate overnight. Preheat broiler. Sprinkle brown sugar on top of custards and place under the hot broiler for 2-3 minutes until sugar melts and caramelizes. Leave for 3-4 hours to cool and set; decorate with mint leaves and serve with fresh fruit.

Serves 6

– GRILLED COCONUT PINEAPPLE –

4 tablespoons unsweetened flaked coconut
1 pineapple
2 tablespoons rum
⅓ cup (2oz/50g) brown sugar

Line a broiler pan with foil and spread coconut over. Broil under a low heat, stirring frequently, until just toasted. Remove and set aside.

Using a sharp knife, cut pineapple, lengthwise, into 8 wedges, cutting right through leaves and leaving them intact. Cut away core. Sprinkle rum evenly over flesh.

Place pineapple wedges in broiler pan and sprinkle brown sugar over. Broil under a medium heat until sugar begins to caramelize and pineapple is hot and beginning to soften. Sprinkle over reserved coconut.

Serves 4

CARIBBEAN CREPES

2 eggs
½ cup (4fl oz/115ml) coconut milk
¾ cup (6fl oz/175ml) milk
1 cup (4oz/115g) all-purpose flour
salt
1 tablespoon superfine sugar
1 tablespoon (½oz/15g) butter, melted
oil, for frying
sifted confectioners' sugar, for dusting
FILLING:
3 tablespoons (1½oz/40g) butter
3 tablespoons light soft brown sugar
4 bananas, sliced
grated rind and juice of 1 orange
3 tablespoons dark rum

In a bowl, whisk together eggs, coconut milk, and milk. Sift flour and salt into a mixing bowl. Stir in sugar. Make a well in center of flour mixture and gradually beat in egg mixture to form a smooth batter. Stir in melted butter.

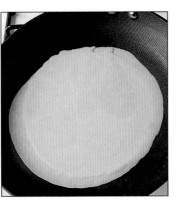

Heat a 8-9in (20-23cm) non-stick skillet and brush with a little oil. Pour in enough batter to coat base of pan, tipping pan so that the base is evenly coated. Cook crêpe until browned underneath and set on top. Turn over and cook other side. Remove from pan and keep warm while cooking remaining batter to make another 7 crêpes.

To make filling, melt butter in a heavy-based skillet and stir in sugar.

Add banana slices and cook, shaking pan frequently, for 1-2 minutes until beginning to soften. Add orange rind and juice, and rum. Boil rapidly, until liquid is well reduced and slightly thickened.

Place a spoonful of banana filling on one quarter of each warm crêpe. Fold crêpes in half over the filling and then into quarters. Arrange 2 crêpes on each plate and dust with sifted confectioners' sugar. Serve immediately.

Serves 4

── SPICE ISLAND CRUMBLE ──

½ cup (4oz/115g) butter
4 firm bananas, cut into 1in (2.5cm) pieces
1 large ripe mango, peeled and cut into chunks
1 ripe papaya, peeled, deseeded, and cut into chunks
4 ripe passion fruit
⅔ cup (5oz/150g) light brown sugar
juice of 1 orange
juice of 1 lime
1¼ cups (5oz/150g) all-purpose flour
1 teaspoon ground cinnamon
¼ teaspoon ground allspice
¼ teaspoon ground cloves
¼ teaspoon freshly grated nutmeg
1⅓ cups (4oz/115g) unsweetened flaked coconut
whipped heavy cream and rum, to serve

Preheat oven to 375F (190C). Use 1 table-spoon (½oz/15g) butter to grease a large, shallow, ovenproof gratin dish. Arrange banana, mango, and papaya pieces in dish. Cut passion fruits in half, scoop out the pulp and seeds, and spread over fruit. Sprinkle with 3 tablespoons of the sugar, pour over orange and lime juices, and gently mix fruit together.

Sift flour, cinnamon, allspice, cloves, and nutmeg into a bowl. Stir in remaining sugar, and coconut. Rub in remaining butter until mixture resembles bread crumbs. Sprinkle over fruit. Bake for 35-40 minutes until fruit is tender and top is brown and crisp. If topping browns too quickly, reduce heat. Stir a little rum into whipped cream and serve with crumble.

Serves 6

EXOTIC FRUIT SALAD

1 small watermelon
1 papaya, peeled, deseeded, and chopped
3 mangosteens
1 small pineapple, peeled, cored, and chopped
4oz (115g) blueberries
3 passion fruit
SYRUP:
⅔ cup (5oz/150g) superfine sugar
juice of 1 lime
rum, to taste (optional)
DECORATION:
strips of lime rind
mint leaves

To make syrup, place sugar and ⅔ cup (5fl oz/150ml) water in a saucepan. Heat gently until sugar has dissolved. Simmer for 5 minutes. Leave to cool. Add lime juice and rum, if using. Cut across watermelon to remove one third. Scoop out seeds and discard. Using a large melon baller, scoop out balls of flesh. Place in a bowl. Add papaya. Cut a zig-zag edge on larger melon shell.

Halve mangosteens, remove fruit and add to bowl with pineapple and blueberries. Halve passion fruit, and scoop pulp and seeds into bowl of fruit, and mix together. Transfer fruit to melon shell. Pour cooled syrup over. Decorate with strips of lime rind and mint leaves.

Serves 6-8

LIME & COCONUT MERINGUE PIE

¼ cup (1oz/25g) cornstarch
1¼ cups (10fl oz/300ml) coconut milk
grated rind and juice of 2 limes
2 large eggs, separated
¾ cup (6oz/175g) superfine sugar
PASTRY:
1½ cups (6oz/175g) all-purpose flour
salt
⅓ cup (3oz/85g) butter
1 teaspoon superfine sugar
1 egg yolk

To make pastry, sift flour and salt into a bowl. Rub in butter to resemble bread crumbs. Add sugar. Mix in egg yolk, adding enough cold water to make a firm dough. On a floured surface, roll out pastry and use to line a 8in (20cm) loose-based quiche pan. Chill for 30 minutes. Preheat oven to 375F (190C). Line pie shell with baking parchment and baking beans. Bake for 15 minutes. Remove paper and beans and return pie shell to oven for 5-10 minutes until cooked. Turn oven down to 325F (170C).

In a saucepan, gradually combine cornstarch with coconut milk. Bring to a boil slowly, stirring constantly. Cook, stirring, for 3 minutes until thickened. Remove from heat and add the lime rind and juice, egg yolks, and ¼ cup (2oz/50g) of the sugar. Pour into pie shell. Whisk egg whites until very stiff then gradually whisk in remaining sugar. Spread egg whites over filling and swirl with a palette knife. Bake for 10-15 minutes until lightly browned. Serve hot or cold.

Serves 6

QUEEN OF PUDDINGS

14fl oz (400ml) can coconut milk
2 tablespoons (1oz/25g) butter
grated rind of 1 lime
2 eggs, separated
¼ cup (2oz/50g) superfine sugar
1½ cups (3oz/85g) fresh white bread crumbs
3-4 tablespoons guava jelly, warmed
shreds of lime rind, to decorate

Butter a 3¾ cup (30fl oz/850ml) oven dish.
Put coconut milk, butter, and grated lime
rind in a saucepan and bring to the boil.
Remove from the heat. In a bowl, whisk
together egg yolks and half the sugar. Pour
in coconut milk mixture. Put bread crumbs
in prepared dish and strain the coconut milk
mixture over. Leave to stand for 20 minutes
for bread crumbs to swell. Preheat oven to
350F (180C). Bake the pudding for
30 minutes until lightly set. Remove from
oven.

Spread guava jelly over pudding. In a bowl,
whisk egg whites until stiff, then whisk in
remaining sugar. Pile on top of pudding.
Bake for a further 10-15 minutes until
meringue is lightly browned. Scatter shreds
of lime rind over and serve.

Serves 4

– CARAMELIZED RICE PUDDINGS –

⅔ cup (4oz/115g) round-grain rice
14fl oz (400ml) can evaporated milk
1¾ cup (14fl oz/400ml) milk
2 tablespoons (1oz/25g) superfine sugar
1 vanilla bean, split lengthwise
1 cinnamon stick
grated rind of ½ orange
⅔ cup (5fl oz/150ml) heavy cream
3 eggs
4 oranges
CARAMEL:
¾ cup (6oz/175g) superfine sugar
⅓ cup (3fl oz/85ml) water

To make caramel, put sugar and water into a small saucepan and heat gently until sugar dissolves.

Bring to the boil and boil gently, without stirring, until the liquid is golden. Remove pan from heat and allow to darken a little more. Divide caramel among 8 ramekin dishes and immediately carefully swirl dishes so that sides are well coated. Set dishes aside on a baking sheet.

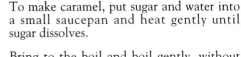

Put rice, evaporated milk, milk, and superfine sugar into saucepan. Add vanilla, cinnamon stick, and grated orange rind. Gently bring to the boil, stirring. Cover, and simmer very gently, stirring occasionally, for 25 minutes until rice is tender.

Preheat oven to 325F (160C). Remove pan
from the heat and allow rice to cool slightly.
Remove vanilla and cinnamon.

In a bowl, whisk together cream and eggs,
then stir into rice. Spoon mixture over
caramel in ramekin dishes. Bake for
30 minutes until firm.

Meanwhile, with a sharp knife, cut away all
the skin and pith from oranges. Cut out
segments by cutting down on either side of
membrane. Reserve any juice and place in a
bowl with the orange segments. Set aside.
Carefully unmold rice puddings on to plates.
Serve immediately with the orange
segments and juice.

Serves 8

—— RUM PUNCH ——

1 cup (8oz/225g) granulated sugar
½ cup (4fl oz/115ml) fresh lime juice
1½ cups (12fl oz/350ml) golden rum
12 ice cubes
Angostura bitters
grated nutmeg
TO DECORATE:
fresh mint
slices of lime

Put granulated sugar and 1 cup (8fl oz/ 225ml) water in a saucepan. Bring slowly to the boil, stirring until sugar has dissolved.

Lower heat and simmer for 3 minutes. Remove from heat and set aside to cool. When completely cold, pour syrup into a jug.

Add lime juice, rum, ice cubes, and 2 cups (16fl oz/450ml) water. Stir well then strain into glasses. Add a dash of Angostura bitters to each glass, and sprinkle with nutmeg. Decorate with mint and lime slices, and serve.

Serves 4

PINA COLADA

crushed ice
2 cups (16fl oz/450ml) fresh pineapple juice
1 cup (8fl oz/225ml) coconut milk
1 cup (8fl oz/225ml) white rum
DECORATION:
pineapple slices
cherries with stalks

Place crushed ice in 4 tall glasses to three-quarters fill.

Pour pineapple juice into a cocktail shaker or large screw-topped jar. Add coconut milk and white rum, and shake vigorously to blend. Pour into glasses over the ice.

To decorate, cut each pineapple slice into quarters and cut a slit half-way through each wedge. Place over rims of glasses. Hang cherries over glass rims and serve immediately.

Serves 4

— TROPICAL PARTY PUNCH —

14oz (400g) can mango slices
¾ cup (6oz/175g) granulated sugar
juice of 4 limes
juice of 4 lemons
⅔ cup (5fl oz/150ml) grenadine
generous 1 cup (9fl oz/250ml) white rum
4½ cups (35fl oz/1 litre) tropical fruit juice
4½ cups (35fl oz/1 litre) lemonade
ice cubes, to serve
TO DECORATE:
slices of orange
slices of lime

Empty mangoes and their syrup into a food processor and process to a purée.

Put granulated sugar and ¾ cup (6fl oz/175ml) water in a saucepan. Bring slowly to the boil, stirring, until sugar has dissolved. Lower heat and simmer for 3 minutes. Remove from heat and set aside to cool.

Add lime and lemon juice, mango purée, grenadine, and rum. Stir well then chill. Just before serving, stir in tropical fruit juice and lemonade. Pour into 2 large jugs filled with ice cubes. Decorate with orange and lime slices.

Makes 16 glasses

— DRIVER'S PINEAPPLE PUNCH —

1 ripe pineapple
1 ripe mango
⅔ cup (5fl oz/150ml) traditional ginger beer
sparkling mineral water
juice of 1 lime

Cut top off pineapple and scoop out flesh, leaving shell intact. Discard core and reserve any juice.

Peel mango and coarsely chop the flesh. Place pineapple pulp and juice to a blender or food processor. Add mango and ginger beer. Process until smooth.

Add sparkling water to thin to a drinking consistency, and add lime juice. Pour punch into pineapple shell to serve.

Serves 2

INDEX